Platinum Publishing

FATIMA OMAR KHAMISSA &
PLATINUM PUBLISHING

Present

BRILLIANCE!

PROFILES OF
EXTRAORDINARY
INNOVATORS,
EXPERTS & LEADERS

Platinum Publishing
c/o Fatima Omar Khamissa
18-3555 Don Mills Road
Suite 131
Toronto
Ontario
M2H 3N3

Like anything in life, there are no guarantees that using the methods mentioned by the publisher by any of the contributors will result in the same success mentioned.

Although the author and publisher have made every effort to ensure that the information in this book was correct at press time, the author and publisher do not assume and hereby disclaim any liability to any party for any loss, damage, or disruption caused by errors or omissions, whether such errors or omissions result from negligence, accident, or any other cause.

The information contained within this book is strictly for educational purposes. If you wish to apply ideas contained in this book, you are taking full responsibility for your actions

ISBN: 978-0-9953136-7-5

Platinum Publishing

TABLE OF CONTENTS

FORWARD

In the past few years I noticed the positive successful Muslim voices have been missing from the media. This bothered me. I didn't like turning on the television or reading news on social media convincing me that all Muslims are bad, all Muslims were terrible, and all Muslims want to hurt other people.

The Muslims around me were amazing people. The Muslims around me are making a difference in the world. The Muslims around me give charity to the orphans and help the weak and the vulnerable.

When I started getting into digital marketing and coaching in the online space, I was introduced to Muslims who were extraordinary in what they were accomplishing online and off-line.

These people touched and inspired me in more ways than I can possibly mention.

So I took the initiative and interviewed each one of them to showcase their achievements, their vulnerabilities, and their secrets to success.

I hope you enjoy this book as much as I did putting it together.

I acknowledge each and every one of the people in this book for their time, their tenacity and their leadership

Love,
Fatima Omar Khamissa
Publisher
March 2020

NASEMA BEGUM

"Success tastes much sweeter once you've failed because you see yourself grow. It's amazing how much you learn. "

F: Welcome to the call Nasema. Let's dive right in; can you tell us about the business that you do and the kind of customers you help?

N: I'm a life coach and I specialize in permissible Dating. I help singles effectively navigate the permissible dating scene so they can meet and marry their soul mate, whilst operating within principles and etiquette. I enable singles to have the marriages they want and to create families that are perfect for them.

Perhaps it would help if I begin by explaining what a life coach is. If you look at it from the perspective of an athlete or a sports star, they all have coaches. For example, a hundred meters runner, the coach will observe them and look at every movement they're making. Then the coach will support and guide the athlete to improve each movement. Each improvement helps to shave off milliseconds from their record. The accumulative effect of these improvements enables them to break their record by running faster and achieving their goals quicker.

As a life coach, I do this in people's personal lives. I help them to take back control of their lives so they are not at the mercy of the people and circumstances in their lives.

What I do is help singles figure out what type of life partner they want, how to speak to singles confidently and build a connection, whether it's on a dating app, marriage event or a family introduction. The structure I provide stops singles feeling overwhelmed at the thought of finding 'the one' in a world with seven billion people. It prevents them from becoming disheartened while they watch their friends get married and have children, while they get left behind.

There are also divorced singles, some of them are parents, and they all want the opportunity to find a life partner, without having to settle. I equip them with tools to deal with their present circumstances because they have concerns, issues or even chaos in their lives, whether it be their family, friends, work, children, finance or health. I help them thrive in that situation rather than to just survive it.

I teach self-love and acceptance no matter what has happened in the past, or where they are now in their lives. It doesn't matter whether they've had permissible or even "not allowed in your faith" relationships they can love and accept themselves for the person they are, without feeling like an outsider. When they learn to accept themselves, then they can accept others for who they are and who they are not.

My approach helps singles to get their energy, joy, and happiness back in their lives, not only do they get things done, it makes them highly attractive to other singles. I help take the fear and stress of the whole situation, making the process a lot easier for them.

F: That's wonderful. Nasema tells us a little bit about the back story. Was there a person that inspired you? Or a book or a movie? What led you up to this field? Most people don't get out of university and say "I want to be a life coach and help women strive and find love." Give us a little bit of the back story of the journey that got you to where you are today.

N: Yes, I never really heard of coaching until a few years ago. I always thought coaching was for people who experienced serious trauma in their lives and they needed professional help to resolve their issues. There was a taboo around using these services because it meant you were a "damaged" person. I believed I was not that kind of person and I didn't need that kind of help, but I became really unhappy. I still thought, "I'm not broken and I don't need to be fixed. I'm not happy in my life but it's okay, I don't need that kind of help"- until I experienced a very difficult time in my life. That's when I started to believe that I had something seriously wrong with me and I had to be fixed quickly. That's where my coaching journey began.

It was more an act of desperation. I was in an abusive marriage and as a result, I was going through a divorce. A few months earlier, I had started a new job and I was being bullied by my manager at work. I had been given a warning for my performance so I was about to lose my job - despite working 9 to 10 hours a day trying to do my best, it still wasn't good enough. I was also diagnosed with clinical depression. I was at rock bottom - I hated myself and I couldn't bear to look at myself in the mirror. I was attending counseling sessions, but they weren't working for me and I just didn't know what to do. I got to a point where I had to make a decision; I decided to take four months off work, deal with my divorce, then return to work and deal with the problems there.

I've always been able to resolve the problems that I've had in my life but this was so overwhelming. Three weeks into these four months I realized I'd become a prisoner in my own home. I actually couldn't leave the house - all I did was cry, eat, try and sleep and watch TV - that's all I did. I finally thought, "I can't carry on doing this. I can't live like this." At the time, you, Fatima, were advertising the Transformational Coaching course. I remember thinking "I had nothing to lose, I've lost my marriage, I am about to lose my job, I need to do something because I can't carry on like this." I felt so desperate. I had nothing else, no other options and so I went for it.

It was the best decision I ever made because the course had a very big impact on my approach to life. I negotiated a new job role with my employer and I got moved to a new team. Once I was back at work, I grew in confidence; I developed my knowledge and abilities, resulting in me being put forward for a talent management program. I'm currently managing a big, high profile project at work. I am divorced. I've lost weight - 1 and a half stones (21 pounds), and I did that all without taking anti-depressants. Today I'm happier than I've ever been. Coaching is what got me to where I am today. I'm building the life I want and it's amazing what coaching can do for you.

I know that when people hear about abuse and abusive relationships, they may immediately think of physical abuse. It's not always just physical abuse and I know to live in the UK, it is defined by the government as "an incidence or pattern of incidents of controlling, coercive, or threatening behavior; violence or abuse between intimate partners or family members". These can include (but are not limited to) psychological, physical, mental, sexual, financial and emotional abuse.

It may not occur to people that those are all types of abuse. When they talk about control, these are acts designed to make a victim dependent on their abuser. So that includes isolating them from the people who could support them; they are exploited for their money and abilities, for the personal gain of their abuser. It's preventing the victim from being independent and closely controlling what they do daily. When it comes to coercive behavior, it includes assaults, threats, humiliation, intimidation or other forms of abuse that are used to harm or punish or frighten the victim.

There needs to be greater awareness and ultimately, changes in perception. A lot of people don't realize they're being abused and that they're in an abusive relationship purely because they're not being physically attacked. That's one of the realizations I had while I was going through the divorce process. I had been in an abusive relationship and I wasn't aware of the danger I was in while I was in that situation. Women can underestimate the severity of the situation because they just think it's going to get better until things escalate.

Let me tell you a bit more about my story. I attended several marriage courses and I was aware a marriage was a contract. I knew I wanted to marry someone that was on the same page as me. I was introduced to a guy by my family and we met up, I asked a lot of questions and I remember hearing his responses and thinking he's the right guy for me. Things moved quickly and whilst arranging the wedding his family started demanding gifts from my family. That was a red flag and a warning sign that I ignored. I convinced myself, thinking, "He's not like that, it's his family. I'm marrying him; I'm not marrying his family, so it'll be okay".

On the day of the marriage, my now ex-husband and I, were making small talk and I asked "how's your job going?" and general conversation about what he was doing. His reply was, "oh I've got something to tell you. I don't work there anymore, I quit my job." It turned out that he didn't even have a steady job and he had no real plans of getting one. I was shocked, I didn't know what to say, and especially when he had assured me that he could financially support me and our future children. At the time, I was 29 years old and I wanted a family. For me, hearing this meant it would be a financial struggle to raise and support a family. I didn't want that for myself because I had watched my parents struggle. I was gutted and felt deceived as I wouldn't have agreed to this marriage had he been honest from the outset. I felt trapped in that situation and I thought "I just married this man, how can I walk away now? I'm married!"

I felt obligated to go through and within hours of moving-in with his family, I found him to be very critical and controlling. Everything had to be done in a particular way and over the next few months more and more lies came out. It was almost like I had married a fictional character. The man I thought I was marrying didn't even exist. I had married a pack of lies. Within a month of being married, he and his family started making demands of me, asking me to quit my job so I could sit at home to cook and clean for them. Next, they asked for £8,000 to replace the central heating - they had a way of asking for things especially when it came to money. They would ask, without really asking you, so you felt obligated to give them what they wanted. It was an odd situation.

They would even restrict me from visiting my family. I was only allowed to visit them every other Sunday for two hours. My ex-husband and I were fighting all the time but I couldn't understand why. His family wasn't happy with the fact that he had two brothers living there so I didn't feel comfortable not being covered up. They weren't happy with the way I dressed and they didn't want me to wear Asian dresses. Instead, they wanted me to wear the traditional sari generally worn by married women. I was told that I was bringing shame to his family because I wasn't dressing the way they expected me to dress. They laughed at me and criticized me; I thought I must be the one in the wrong. So I tried to be the daughter-in-law they wanted me to be and I tried to keep them happy. But the more time went on, the more unpredictable my ex-husband became. It came to the point where the arguments and his family's demands got too much for me, and I left their home.

After several months of trying to reconcile and talking to the in-laws, I decided to give the marriage one more try. I thought that maybe I hadn't tried hard enough. Maybe I was in the wrong, maybe I should have behaved differently and maybe I should have been more understanding. So I started blaming myself for the whole thing. However, as soon as I stepped back into his family home, I knew it was a big mistake. His behavior was worse than ever. There was a lot of tension and they imposed more rules on me and even though I followed them, they still weren't happy. The arguments got more and more intense and his behavior becomes threatening. His family was forcing him to decide on ending the marriage and he couldn't decide what he wanted.

As the situation continued to escalate, he called my parents insulting them and arguing with them over the phone. His family got an extended family member involved, who also started calling my parents and insulting them. I contacted the local imam at the mosque to help us.

The whole time I was told,

"Be patient and it'll work out" or

"It's your fault" or

"You should've done things differently."

I was also told, "If the marriage ends you're the woman, you'll be stigmatized so it's your problem."

This is what generally happens in the Bangladeshi community; the woman is blamed for the breakdown of her marriage and she becomes a second class citizen.

I was in a crazy situation where I didn't want the marriage, yet at the same time, I didn't want a divorce and be treated like a second class citizen. I didn't want to be seen as the bottom-of-society. I blamed myself because I shouldn't have married him and I thought I deserved it. The situation continued and then one day I overheard his family discussing in the kitchen; I could hear them talking about how to end the marriage and what options were available including involving the police. I was really scared for myself as the situation was escalating further. I spoke to the Imam, and he turned a blind eye.

A few days later I found myself in another argument. This time, his family called the police.

Before I could comprehend what had happened, I found myself being arrested for assaulting my ex-husband and I spent that night in a police cell. That was my deepest darkest moment. It was the longest night of my life. I felt humiliated and worthless, I couldn't bear to face the consequences of this arrest. Not only was I going to be a divorced woman, but I was also going to have a criminal record. I didn't want to live anymore, I hated myself, I hated my life, I couldn't understand why this would happen to me and yet …I felt I deserved it.

That night I realized how alone I was; no one could help me and no one could save me. God was the only one who could help me and He was the only one who could get me out of this situation. That night, my relationship with God changed and I truly recognized how dependent I am on Him.

Needless to say, I wasn't charged because there was no assault. My experience shows the extent an abuser will go to just to get their way. My abusers used the police, who are there to protect the vulnerable, as an extension of their abuse towards me.

Today as I look back, I'm so grateful that my marriage ended. It was the best thing that could have happened to me. I never, ever thought I would say that - but it was.

The ending of my marriage saved me from a life of misery.

God has given me a second chance to live a life that matters, to live a life of possibility, a life where I fulfill my dreams.

From my experience, I have learned that there are so many women out there being abused and they have little or no help. I sought help from an imam, he tried his best and I am grateful for his help. What I also realized was that the imam is not trained to be marriage counselors or mediators, yet we expect them to fulfill that role.

This is my story and how I started life coaching. I want to empower singles be powerful and effective in finding their life partner and to create a family that is perfect for them, and who are ambassadors for the next generation.

 I do this so singles are not trapped by societal rules and beliefs. I want them to be amazing contributors to society, to fulfill their dreams.

F: Wow that's a pretty amazing story, thanks for sharing. And if there's a woman out there reading this and she's in a violent, abusive relationship what are some of the obstacles that are preventing her from getting out and living that life, that amazing life that she gets to create?

N: What it boils down to is fear; the fear of the unknown, the fear of criticism, the fear of not being good enough or worthy enough, the fear of upsetting her loved ones, fear of rejection by her friends and family and the fear of failure in their new life. They also have worries about finances; how will they support themselves, especially if there are children involved. What if their children are taken away from them, where are they going to live? Who's going to be there to support them through this? That's what stops women from actually stepping out of that situation.

These fears are the thoughts that cripple us and stop us from taking action. Our mind shows us what can potentially happen, the worst-case scenario, as a way to keep us safe. It doesn't mean these thoughts will become a reality. When we listen to these thoughts, it stops us from taking action. We remain in these abusive situations, hoping things get better, underestimating the danger we may be in. When we talk to friends and family about our situation, there may be some support, but at the same time, they can put more doubt and uncertainty in your head because they're telling you about their own fears and thoughts.

Before you know it, we've accepted our situation, we feel trapped and we pray and hope something happens to change our circumstances. We wait for a lucky break where everything will fall into place, but that never comes.

You have to create it yourself.

You do that by deciding what you want, creating a plan and following through on it. You have to do this despite the fear and the screaming negative thoughts in your head. You have to take action. Once you do that, you will find doors and opportunities start opening up to help your plans come to fruition.

F: Yes I agree. Fear can be very crippling. Nasema, what does a woman who has all this fear in her head do to successfully achieve the life that she wants? How can she beat that obstacle, go around it and help herself provide a solution for her pain?

N: I use the 'Review and Revive' toolkit. This toolkit can be used by singles too. It looks at where you are now and where you want to go. This could be an emotional state such as peace of mind or wanting to remarry, a physical state such as moving home. The toolkit will help to give you renewed strength, self-belief and desire to achieve the outcome that you want. It will help you to build yourself up to take the actions that you need to take. There are four steps, and you can start with any step that you feel most comfortable with. Once you have a routine, then choose another step and add that to your routine, until you are completing all four steps every day.

Step 1: Journaling

We have so many thoughts and emotions going through our heads every day. Journaling gets those thoughts and emotions out of your head, giving you the release to be able to think clearly?

When you are journaling, think about any surprises, upsets or disappointments that you may have experienced that day and write them down on a piece of paper. This in itself is a therapeutic process, it helps to relieve the stresses of that day. It also helps you deal with traumas and emotions you are experiencing.

I recommend journaling every day for 20 to 30 minutes writing your thoughts.

Step 2: Affirmations

Affirmations are positive statements that help to change and remove specific behaviors and thoughts.

There's a saying that goes "you are what you think", meaning your actions are based on the thoughts you're having. An affirmation helps you to change negative thoughts. It rewires your brain and changes the perception that you have of yourself and your situation. As a result, you're able to counteract any negative thoughts, leading you to take different actions resulting in powerful outcomes.

Try these affirmations:

- I am the architect of my life. I build its foundations and I choose its contents.

- My life partner is waiting for me

- My body is healthy, my mind is brilliant and my soul is tranquil.

- I have an endless talent that I will begin to use today.

- I forgive those who have harmed me. I peacefully detach from them.

- Happiness is a choice, I base my happiness upon my accomplishments and the blessings I have been given.

- My ability to conquer my challenges is limitless. My potential to succeed is infinite.

You can change these affirmations to what you need right now and what you want to achieve. To see changes, you must repeat your affirmation three times a day. I recommend putting these affirmations as a reminder on your phone, setting them for the morning, noon, and evening. On each occasion repeat the affirmation three times. This must be done consistently to see changes in you.

Step 3: Exercising

We hear a lot about exercise being beneficial, however, a lot of people struggle with it. I do highly recommend it because it changes the way you're feeling. When you exercise your body, you release a hormone called serotonin. Serotonin improves your mood and makes you feel more positive, especially when you're going through a very difficult time in your life. You need to be in a positive state as often as you can, you never know when you will bump into your life partner. Being in a positive state allows you to take positive actions.

The best thing to do is go to the gym but if you can't, then try the following:

- Get off the train or bus a stop earlier and walk home or to the office

- Take the stairs instead of the elevator

- Go to the local park and walk around the perimeter of the park

- When you're walking, speed walk so it becomes a workout

- If you're at work, physically approach colleagues and talk to them, rather than sending an email or calling them

Doing all of that should help you to relieve stress, improve your memory, help you sleep better and even if you're feeling tired, it will give you a boost of energy. It will equip you with the ability to face challenges in life and healthily cope with them.

Step 4: Gratitude Journal

Take 10 minutes out of your day to write down everything you're grateful for. Include at least three things that happened on that particular day. For example, if you're running late but still managed to get to work on time, or you completed a task sooner than you expected. This will have an amazing impact on the way that you feel and it will change your perspective of your situation, making it easier to tackle difficult issues.

F: I want to know about your mind. Were you always a big thinker? Did you have these big crazy amazing beliefs that you were going to help women and children all over the world? Did you need to change your beliefs and your mindsets to get to who you are today?

N: Growing up we didn't have a lot of money. My parents worked hard and they worked long hours. My dad worked in a garment factory, he used to bring work home with him and my mum would help him out. They were doing all this whilst also trying to raise four children. My dad eventually bought his garment factory. My siblings and I used to help out when he bought work home. We would go to school, come home from school, go to Quran classes and then help my parents at home. So I grew up with an amazing work ethic.

Watching my parents as I was growing up taught me to push myself and do more with my time. I found my dad inspiring because he was the most successful man I knew. We grew up around poverty and a lot of my neighbors didn't have work. My dad would employ these individuals to work for him, teaching them new skills so they could improve the quality of their lives.

I knew I wanted to be somebody who made an impact on the world.

I didn't know how but I had these great aspirations of being a successful entrepreneur and I still have that. What happens is, you go through life and we all have these dreams and ambitions. Then life happens to you, you start believing others' opinions of you, that you don't deserve success or you're not worthy of it. You try something and it fails then you become fearful and stop trusting your own decisions and your ability. Before you know it, you've stopped taking action.

You hold yourself back, talking yourself out of great ideas. I've seen others act upon the same ideas and they are doing well. My divorce has made me more determined than ever to achieving my dreams. It can take time to change your mindset. Coaching has given me amazing techniques and great tools to help change my thoughts. When you change your mindset, you change the outcome of your life. If you want to change something in your life, you have to change your approach to that specific area or task. Like Einstein said, "insanity is doing the same thing over and over again and expecting different results." This is what I was doing - I kept doing more of the same, thinking the result would be different each time, but it wasn't.

I'd recommend following the 'Review and Revive' toolkit, just a few minutes every day and you'll see a change in the way you think and feel. You'll see the changes in the results you have in your life.

We only have one life so we need to go for it and live life to the fullest. You don't know when we won't be here anymore or when our last day will be - so just go for it! Fight the fear and do it anyway.

F: I agree. Thomas Edison said that he didn't fail 10,000 times, he found 10,000 ways that didn't work. Share with us how failure helped you to grow, to become the incredible woman that you are today.

N: Growing up I always thought success was carrying out a few tasks, working hard and if everything went to plan and you got the results you needed, then that was a success. Every time my plans didn't work out, I labeled myself as a failure and I gave up. Over time, I lost confidence in my abilities and I found myself fearful of taking action.

Through coaching, I realized that I was always in a place of fear. I was scared I would fail and so I didn't work on achieving my goals and dreams. What I've learned is that failure is part of success. Every time I fail it's an opportunity to learn. When we have the success we celebrate, but when we have a failure we should stop and reflect.

Failing helped me figure out what went wrong. I learned from my mistakes, I adapted and took a different approach so that I wouldn't repeat my mistakes. That's when I got success. Success tastes much sweeter once you've failed because you see yourself grow. It's amazing how much you learn. I believe true success is the growth and learning you get from failing.

F: If you had a chance, what would you say to your younger self?

N: What I would say to my younger self is:

- Don't wait for successes and achievements in life to just happen. Don't wait for your life to fall into place because it doesn't work like that. You must decide what you want and go out there and make it happen.

- Be clear about what you want to achieve in your life. Find someone who has the results you want, ask them to coach you and model their actions to achieve their success. This will prevent you from repeating their mistakes and achieve your goals faster.

- Don't worry about what could happen or what could go wrong, just go out there and work on achieving your dreams. If something does go wrong, deal with it when it happens. Don't worry about it now as it may never happen.

- As you get older you'll notice how quickly times goes by, so make your time on this earth count. Life's too short to waste it so have a plan for everything you do. Keep taking action every day, even if it's a very small task.

- Don't doubt yourself or your judgment because you are the only one who knows what you want and what's right for you. Don't let other people and their opinions divert you from your path.

- You're not responsible for other people's happiness. There's a saying "you can please some of the people some of the time but you can't please all of the people all of the time." Do what makes you happy and you will have a productive and fulfilling life.

- Learn; never stop learning because life is about growth. Learn continuously, implement what you've learned and share it with others.

F: That's great advice. Master Coach Tony Robbins talk about rituals and habits that can break you or rituals and habits that can propel you into success. Give us a little snippet of the private Nasema and some of the habits and rituals that you participate in?

N: I use the 'Review and Revival' toolkit I spoke about earlier. I journal daily, and it helps to put into perspective what happened that day. It helps me think through what I need to do and what my next steps will be.

I exercise at least three times a week - I have set days that I attend the gym. This helps me to maintain a routine. I also have plans listing all my tasks for the next three months, so I know exactly what I'm going to be working on and what the deadlines are. I have dedicated time slots where I get focused and get things done.

When I achieve my target I like to treat myself even if it's something really small, to celebrate that success. It keeps me going and keeps me motivated. Every morning I remind myself why I work on my business because I want to help women and empower them. This work also helps me prepare for the Hereafter and this has become a powerful reminder for me. That's what propels me forward and keeps that desire in my heart to help people. I know that not only do they benefit but I benefit also.

F: Nasema, let's get back to that young woman who needs your help. Either she is in an abusive relationship, or she's just feeling stuck in her life. What would be your best piece of advice for her?

N: What I would say to her is, you need to take action towards what you want, and that action will give you relief because you have finally responded to that feeling inside. The fact that you are feeling yearning inside you means that there's more for you to give, and your current situation is keeping you stuck. That yearning is not going to stop until you do something about it. So decide what you want and find a coach who has achieved the results you want. Follow their advice and their guidance and you will achieve your goal. Don't think that you have to do it on your own because this will create reasons and excuses as to why you can't do it. Your mind will tell you not to do it, there may be people around you who will tell you not to do it, or you might convince yourself you don't have what it takes. So you have to fight those thoughts and take action.

F: Wonderful. Nasema if somebody is listening to this and they want to get in touch with you and get information, what's the best way for them to learn about your services or contact you? A phone number or email address? Any kind of social media links that you can share?

N: Yes, I'd love to connect I have a Facebook group called Permissible Dating Coach

And Instagram @nasemabegum so please come and join the group.

I can also be contacted by email at info@nasemabegum.com

ABOUT THE AUTHOR

Nasema was eager to please her parents and grew up to be a well behaved, self-sacrificing individual who consistently tried to keep everyone happy. She grew up in a community that restricted women's role in life to cooking, cleaning, getting married and having children.

Nasema aspired to do more and be more, but her desire to make her parents proud was overwhelming, so she suppressed her ideas and ambitions. However there was one thing she was determined to get, that was an education. Despite her parent's reservations, she went to university and studied BA in Business. She became the first person in her family to ever get a degree.

Nasema went on to get a job and was quickly promoted. However, she felt dissatisfied with her life. She thought that life was about surviving your job and coping with your family issues. Nasema went on to get married, only to find her 'trapped' in an abusive situation. Nasema started coaching as a desperate attempt to help her deal with the darkest moment of her life.

Nasema is now happily divorced and grateful for the opportunities her divorce has given her- the chance to start again, to create a new life for herself and to achieve her dreams. Nasema has a renewed zest for life which is directly attributable to her coaching experience and her passion now is to help women transform their lives so they can live life on their terms.

As the Permissible Dating Coach, Nasema supports singles navigate the permissible dating scene. She brings new approaches to 'find the one' whilst following the Islamic principles and etiquette. She enables singles to have the marriage and the family life they want.

Notes: ✍

CÈLIN MONIQUE CHILDS

"Even when failure and misfortune strikes, you must continue your journey. Most people won't see your vision and they will do everything to keep you from it. Push through, press on, success awaits you at the other end."

Fatima: It is so wonderful to have you here with us. Tell us about what business you are doing and what types of customers you help.

Celin: I have a few businesses. I'll start with my first business. It is called Ruth & Mae's Natural Products. My products are designed for people who have curly hair and want to use natural skin and hair care products. Most of my customers are women who have decided to do a big chop, meaning that they no longer want perms, dyes, and chemicals in their hair. These women shave off or cut down their hair low to get rid of all of the chemicals and the horrible products they've been using over the years. Allowing them to start with a fresh new head of hair.

They want it to grow naturally and to see how long and beautiful it can grow on its own. I design products to help them with this process and to grow their hair naturally without any harsh chemicals as most store-bought products contain. My products are chemical-free, natural and organic. Many people with naturally curly hair often have the burden of it becoming dry and broken. I noticed that the same problem is universal, so I develop products that will keep moisture and oils in the hair naturally so that the hair doesn't break off. It's a real struggle, especially for people who have tight curly hair that dries out easily.

Not very many people on the planet, except mostly those of African descent, have really dry, tight curly hair and so it's a hard process to take care of, especially for women who have been straightening their hair most of their lives. As they transition to natural, I want to be there to provide them with products that will help in the process.

I also make products for people who have really dry skin or those who are trying to get healthier skin. My Ruth & Mae's Natural Skin Products help them heal their skin and keep a beautiful layer of it all the time. That's what I do. That's my first business.

I also have an online course where I show others how to start their product lines. I show people how to go from 0-3 products in six weeks. They have the choice to start a haircare, skincare, or makeup line. My goal is to help at least 1,000 people start their product line and leave a legacy for their families. The course is designed to simplify the process of developing a product line, even if it's on a budget.

This course is designed for people who want to start a business from the comfort of their own homes but may not know where to start. I started mixing products in my kitchen and I started my Ruth & Mae's business on my own, without any guidance. I had a dream of having my product line so I taught myself how to make a store and grow my business. I started with two products. My hair-growth sprays. I started with these two products for three years. Today I currently have over a dozen products in my line. I continue to develop new products for Ruth & Mae's brand and hoping to add some make-up to the line soon.

Entrepreneurship can be easy. I know many people staying at home raising their children. I know that it is extremely important for them to have the opportunity to be with their family and also to worship. Many people who have an entrepreneurial spirit have a passion for something of their own. Maybe it's sewing, its fashion, and maybe its artwork. Maybe they want to start a business from their passions.

I developed the Build Your Product Line Course for the sister who wants to do something from home. It is also designed for the sister who may be tied up in a 9-5 job and she's contributing to her household as I have been for so many years. I'm an entrepreneurial mom. I was a teacher at a private school for nearly a decade. I now enjoy being a full-time entrepreneur, helping and teaching others how to start their entrepreneurial journey. It was important for me to have the ability to spend time with my family and also give them a great enriching life filled with travel, education, and possibilities.

I know some sisters want to give their children a certain lifestyle, they want to be able to send their kids to schools but they don't have the means to pay for it, so they settle and send their kids to public or they choose to home school instead. They may want to travel as I do with my children, they may want to buy the larger home or be able to have a decent car for their family. They may want to be able to give their children the life of their dreams.

My course is for the one who wants to start a business from the ground up or they already have a business and they want to find out how to grow it. My 6-week Build Your Product Line course, will give them that push and give them guidance on how to develop an idea, get going with it and then get their venture up and running. As I continue on my journey, I will be developing larger courses such as how to develop digital products, homeschooling courses for children, and a course to guide sisters who want to build their brands and coach others.

I know there are a lot of sisters out there who want to help other sisters. They've been through divorces, they've overcome fitness and health issues and they can help other sisters who need guidance. Just women who want to help women in business and I have come across a lot of sisters who want to get into coaching. I want to be able to guide them along the way so that they can start their coaching businesses as well.

F: Tell us what led you into the field of making kitchen products and softening products? How did you get started?

C: Back in 2011, I had gone natural for a while but my hair wasn't growing well. The products I used from the store weren't doing my hair any justice. That is when I started researching different ingredients to help with hair growth. Finally, I came up with this concoction called Peppermint Kiss Hair Growth Spray. I would spray my hair at least twice per day and I started to see a huge difference in the moisture that my hair was retaining. I was impressed with how healthy my hair was and how it was starting to grow. One of the ingredients I put in my hair growth sprays, for instance, is MSM; which is natural sulfur. What's amazing is our bodies make MSM, but when we are lacking this substance, our hair is the first thing that takes a hit. My product has MSM in it which will put the sulfur back into the scalp and help the hair grow as it goes back into the body.

My friends started to say, "What are you doing to your hair?" I said, "Well I'm making my concoctions;" and they said, "I'll buy it from you if you give me some." I said, "Really?" A light bulb came on and I started selling it to my friends. Then I said to myself. I am going to make me a website and I'm going to sell this stuff to people online. I always giggle when I think of it because it wasn't the best site. It was a little raggedy website that I had made up. It's still online and I still go back to it from time to time just to see how far I've come. I put this website up and I started to promote it on Facebook and run a couple of Facebook ads to it and I started making sales. I was like "Whoa!" Over three years I sold only Peppermint Kiss♥ and Lavender Kiss♥ Hair Growth Sprays. I would go to different hair expos and vendor events and I would sell this spray. I knew the whole time that eventually, I did want to expand my product line; but I didn't have the money. I wasn't making enough, I had kids, and I am just a teacher. I just didn't make a lot. I was saving so that I could eventually branch out and do more products. So in 2014, I added several new products to the line and rebranded Peppermint Kiss to Ruth & Mae's.

Ruth is my grandmother and Mae is her baby sister. Mae was my oldest living aunt at the time. She was almost 90 years old when for her permission to name my business after her and my grandmother, and she said that I could. It has been an honor. I wanted Ruth & Mae's to be like a natural remedy/vintage brand with a modern twist. I want the products to feel like they came from the home remedies and that old-time feel. Everything smells like something you could eat. From my Cocoa Mint Hair Cleansing Tea to my Whipped Mint Chocolate Hair Mask, whatever you get your hands on, you'll be sure to want to eat it too. You can now find my products online, in the Colorado Country Store and Shai Naturals Store in Colorado, USA.

F: What do you think is stopping a woman from achieving success? What's holding her back?

C: I think there are a few things that are holding her back. The first thing is the fear that she might fail. I know that feeling because I have been there. But there came a time when I said to myself, "I don't care if I fail, I don't care. I'm going to keep getting back up until I succeed. I won't give up."

Your mindset has to change when it comes to wanting to be successful. That successful entrepreneurial woman will be bombarded by others who will disapprove of what she's doing. She has to be strong and prepare for it. I think one thing that helped me prepare was to tell myself I don't care what anybody else thinks of me. I am just going to do it and go for it and not let anyone stop me. My conversion to Islam

12 years ago hit my family quite hard. They completely didn't understand what I was doing so I went through a rough time in sticking with my plan. You have to have the same mindset when it comes to starting a business.

> You have to say "I don't care what anybody says, I am going to do this. I'm going to be an entrepreneur."

F: What are the other obstacles that are holding her back?

C: The other obstacle is that she may be afraid to take a financial risk. She's afraid to say that I am going to invest my money into this business. The devil always has a way of coming in and giving us a poverty mindset. He instills fear in us to make us feel like if we give or use our money to enhance our lives or the lives of others, that we will become poor. People in her life, who have that scarcity and poverty mindset, are going to tell her that she's crazy. She's probably already telling herself that she's crazy for thinking of taking a financial risk. One thing that I encourage new entrepreneurs to do is to put aside money before jumping into opportunities. Just putting aside some money to invest in business takes the edge off of the risk. That way, she's not tapping into her grocery or bill money. Just preparing her. If she's not prepared and she just wants to leap into something, it's going to hold her back. You always have to prepare for it.

F: What do you tell your clients and what did you do for yourself to successfully achieve that outcome and break through the barriers?

C: I think financial risk is a concern for most people. They say I just don't have the money. They want it but they say I don't have, you have to figure out a way to go and get what you want. If you want to have coaching and you want the best, you need to go out and get the money. Go and work, go clean some houses, sell some old or new junk around the house. Do what you have to do to get it. Don't let anything hold you back because if you do, you won't achieve it. You're going to tell yourself I'll get it tomorrow or I'll do it tomorrow. You have to figure out how I can get it done today because we're not promised tomorrow. That's what I had to tell myself. Even when I have to invest in myself it's not just investing money. It's investing in my knowledge and investing in my time.

Another thing that women say that holds them back, and I was going to mention this but I forgot, is their children and their duties as a wife or a mom. They say they don't have the time to execute it. You have to work your business while the kids are at school and while they are napping. You have to do what you have to do. You can't let anything hold you back. You just got to go do it. Like Yoda says, "There is no try, only do!"

F: What happened to you in your life as you were growing up? How did you change your mind and create the beliefs that you have today?

C: Wow that's a good question. Like I said I've always had an entrepreneurial mindset even when I was a little girl. That's always been in me. I think for me the turning point was when I became a Muslim. Maybe a year or two before I became a Muslim, I was really into directing videos and directing movies and I was going to school for that. I wanted to be successful and I said, "I'm going to do this no matter what." I went through a rough time of people bombarding me and telling me that what I was doing was wrong. I knew in my heart that it was right and I think God was shaping me to be strong. No matter what people said, my inner self knew that I was going to be successful if I continued on God's path. I think that was the biggest turning point in my life. I learned that if I know something is good for me then I should go for it.

If it's going to harm me and people are telling me I should leave this, then I can listen. But if it's something that I know is good for me and I can see the vision, then I know I must carry on. If I can see myself standing before God and He is pleased with me, then I know I must stay on this path.

If I can see my vision of the life I want to have, I will do anything to achieve it. Even now people say "What is she doing? Why is she always on the computer? What is she up to?" They can't see my vision but I can see it. When I became a Muslim, God began molding me to be strong. Always remember that when you see your vision, you must do whatever it takes to attain it. You have to also remember that you're really in this life by yourself and you will stand before God by yourself. You have to do what is right for you and that's what I am doing. I hope that made sense.

F: That's a great response. How has failure, obstacles and falling, helped you grow and be the woman you are today?

C: I have failed so many times. Even recently, things weren't wonderful. I remember having $20 in my account and three kids at home. Now I have four kids. Imagine going a week with only $20 in your bank account. One day I woke up and the anxiety and stress of failing overpowered me. The pain of not being able to give my children the life I wanted for them. Wanting my children to be a part of things and they couldn't because I couldn't afford it. That woke me up and I said, "I'm not going to let this happen anymore. I have to do whatever it takes."

I have these four beautiful children and I cannot fail. I think all of us have seen different kinds of pain. Many successful people had to pull themselves up after they felt that pain. When you feel that anxiety and stress, you don't want to ever feel it again. That's when you wake up and do whatever you can to move forward. This pain can either make or break a person. Those who are successful are the ones that push through it. It's the pain that pushes you. That's what pushed me. I knew that I never wanted to feel it ever again. I said I'm too old for this and I got too many kids to only have $20 in my pocket. I have to do something. I can't go through this anymore. That's what pushed me. That's what caused me to move forward and change my course.

F: What would you say to young 18-year-old Celin?

C: I would say girl you better start your business right now. What are you waiting for? By the time you are 40, you will have made it. I was doing so many unbeneficial things, and they weren't helping me to be a better person. I would tell her that she is beautiful and she can accomplish anything and not to let anyone hold her back. I really would. I would tell her to get started on her business now! I've always had the entrepreneurial spirit and I've always been a hustler. I would have car washes as a little kid, Kool-Aid stands, and we were trying to sell fingernail polish and candy bars, just so we could go to the amusement park. I would tell her to pull it together and stop working for people and get your own thing going. I see so many kids now who are starting their businesses. These millennials are starting and retiring before they're 30. It's amazing! I would tell myself to do the same.

F: What are the rituals and habits that you do privately? The habits that propelled you into the success and mindset, the financial success?

C: My private rituals are my salads and taking the time to ask God every single day to help me. I try to be constantly in a state of humbleness, begging Him to guide me in the right direction and do good deeds. That's the key right there. Just asking of God, focusing on the Holy Book, making my prayers. Also giving charity and making sure that I am not withholding. I don't do a lot of things for myself, a lot of it goes to my kids and I just rather take care of people than worry about myself. Those are just things that I think have helped me. I continue to grow and I continue to train. I'm always trying to learn because I am a teacher at heart. I believe in gaining knowledge. I love listening to different podcasts, I read lectures, take courses, and I am just gaining knowledge. I also listen to you Fatima. Those are my keys.

F: If there's a woman out there who wants to start her business, what's the most important thing she should do?

C: The most important thing is she should plan her venture before leaping. She needs to sit down, be patient with the process and she needs to plan out exactly what she wants to do. Sitting down and writing a business plan and thinking about her ideas. Understanding what she's passionate about. You don't want to get into business and just do it because you just want money. You want to do something that you love and that you're going to be helping others with. Just sitting down and planning and understanding what it's going to take is the key. Taking in the whole entrepreneurial experience and understanding the risks, the possible successes, and the hard work that she will have to put in. Some people think that they can run a business for free. This is possible but growing that business for free will be very difficult. I strongly believe that you need to be prepared financially and mentally to avoid setbacks. You have to plan everything. Plan it out. That's my major thing.

F: Celin how can people find out more about you? What's the best way online where they can find you?

C: celinmonique@gmail.com to contact me at www.buildyourownproductline.com to access my Build Your Product Line Course www.ruthandmaes.com to purchase my natural hair and skin care products.

ABOUT THE AUTHOR

Celin Monique Childs is the CEO of Ruth & Mae's Natural Products and an online branding strategist in the United States. She is currently a full-time entrepreneur. Celine's entrepreneurial journey started at a young age washing cars and selling candy. Fast forward to 2011, Celin began making her natural hair care product called Peppermint Kiss and selling it online.

In 2014, she added several new natural products and rebranded the company to Ruth & Mae's, named after her grandmother and her grandmother's baby sister. Currently, she continues to grow her product line and develop new natural products for naturals worldwide. She is a guest instructor in the Business Launch Academy online course, international speaker, founder of The Golden Muslim Course and Brand, and she currently focuses on helping other entrepreneurs brand themselves through social media platforms.

For more information on Celin Monique Childs please visit her website at www.buildyourownproductline.com or visit her online store at www.ruthandmaes.com

Notes:

Notes: ✍

AAQIB AHMED

"Take risks and get out there. You only live once"

Fatima: Let's start with your business Aaqib. What you do and what are the types of customers do you help?

Aaqib: I focus on Facebook marketing. I help entrepreneurial Muslims get more likes, more engagements on Facebook, and get more sales through Facebook marketing.

F: What got you into the field?

A: I wanted to make a difference in people's lives. I was on social media anyway so I was like "how can I make a difference and also monetize my passion as well?"

I did a lot of volunteer work helping a lot of different organizations grow their likes and monetize their blogs to their service or products on Facebook.

Then I said "there is a big need for this. There needs to be more entrepreneurial Muslims who want to be their own boss and Facebook is such a powerful platform to interact and meet people, and makes a difference as well".

Facebook has over 1 billion users and the users spend over 500 million minutes on there every month.

There are multi-billion dollar companies on Facebook. I decided to leverage off it. I wanted to teach other people how to maximize from it as well.

F: What do you think is the most common obstacle preventing the reader, from achieving the kind of outcome that they want from Facebook?

A: The biggest obstacle is the mindset of people. People come onto Facebook to socialize. It's like the world. It's like your offline life where you are just socializing and having a good time. You waste a lot of time. You play Farmville or different pointless games.

If you come on Facebook with a purpose; to leave a legacy, to achieve freedom, to make a difference in people's lives then it gives you that different mindset. Mindset is the most important thing. 95% of people come on Facebook just to socialize and waste their time. It's basically about framing it in a different way and the way people frame Facebook is a socializing tool. It can't really do much, but you can actually build a career from Facebook and make a difference in people's lives, and build a successful business through Facebook marketing as well.

F: What did you need to do when this came into your mind? Because normal average middle-class families, don't grow up with that kind of mindset. Was your family entrepreneurial millionaires? Or were there certain things that you needed to change with your habits, your attitudes, and your beliefs to create this Facebook marketing business that you are doing right now?

A: The biggest thing is building a community, building an eco-system of people around you who are like-minded, who have the same interests as you.

My family was not rich. I come from a humble background - just a normal British Pakistani family. My father used to sell TV's. He used to get TV's from the dump and get them fixed by his friend Peter who was an electrical engineer. He hustled and he persevered. His hands would go bad and he sold TV's for nearly a decade selling them in the newspaper, advertising. He taught me about being an entrepreneur and being a business-focused person to provide for your family.

F: What change did you have to do to go from that humble-mindset to saying "the sky is the limit"? Share that with us.

A: The biggest shift was just asking myself "can I work a 9-5 shift for the next 40 years? And make my boss richer?" I was working in telesales selling bankcard terminals to business owners. I said "I can't be doing this for the rest of my life. God surely made me for a much higher purpose" and that was the big shift. I realized I couldn't be making peanuts every month. It's crazy that what I was making for a month back then, around 1000 pounds or 1500 dollars a month, I can easily make that in a day now. It's crazy.

We know from the history of Islam, from the legacy that came to us now in our generation that Muslims have a high standard. They were very entrepreneurial as well so we have to follow Islam and be more focused on that legacy.

F: So you've changed your attitude, you felt like you couldn't do this for 40 years. What did you do to change?

A: I changed my way of thinking and I changed my company as well. It's all about changing your company and having the right mindset as well. It's about being around "A-players" and changing my company from people who wanted to be in the 9-5 and be around more entrepreneurial people.

F: What's the most important thing that the readers should think of if they want to be entrepreneurs?

A: The ultimate thing they need to know is their passion. Think about what wakes you up in the morning, that one thing you're good at. For me, it started with poetry. I used to be an Islamic poet and from there I realized that I can do much bigger things. I had a following, I was reaching millions of people, and I can't stay in poetry. I need to branch out to personal development or entrepreneurship and so I branched out there. It's all about following your instincts. What are you born to do? What did God put you on this earth for? You are not here to just sell socks in a corner shop.

> You are here to make a difference. It's about finding what your true purpose is in life and being more entrepreneurial so you can achieve freedom and make money.

F: What is your favorite part about being a Facebook marketer?

A: My favorite part is the freedom and the flexibility to work. I can work in my pajamas, I can be working when I am at the lake. I am not stuck to a schedule, I can choose my schedule, and work with whoever I want and when I want. It's amazing. It's having fun, control and freedom.

F: What do you think your customers are doing when not using Facebook?

A: The main thing that people are not doing is - they are not monetizing their Facebook page effectively. A lot of entrepreneurial Muslims have a Facebook page, they gain a following. I've been in a position where you work hard but you're still broke and struggling. They need a follow-up, a face with a card. Drive to the page with free content and start monetizing their Facebook page as soon as possible because then you can invest more money into your Facebook marketing efforts and build the ground on Facebook, reach more people, and have a bigger impact. Organically there's only so much you can do but if you have paid to advertise on Facebook it's more scalable, more trackable, and you can reach a lot more people quickly as well.

F: If the reader wants to know more about you, what's the best and most efficient way for them to get more information about what you do?

A: The best thing to do is just to look me up on Facebook. Aaqib Ahmed or go onto my website www.entrepreneurialmuslim.com and you can find out more information about me.

F: Any last thoughts that you want to share with the readers?

A: Just take risks and get out there. You only live once. To start a business with what you are passionate about and be around like-minded people who are "A-players", entrepreneurial, and just go for it. You don't want to be working the 9-5 for too long. Get out of your comfort zone, set up a Facebook page and just go for it.

ABOUT THE AUTHOR

Aaqib Ahmed is the founder of Entrepreneurial Muslim. A pioneering brand that helps Muslims start a business through Facebook marketing. Across his top students in total within 12 months over a Million dollars has been made in sales. He's worked with leading Muslim brands like AlMaghrib to Bayyinah to Productive Muslim to Islam Channel and many others.

You can find him at EntrepreneurialMuslim.com

Notes:

ABE ARABI

"From 9-5 to Amazon Success"

Abe Arabi; a father, a son, a husband, who was frustrated with the corporate world and decided that he wanted to open an Amazon business. In a short time of three months, we were able to generate $100,000 trying to ditch his 9-5 lifestyle so he could have more options for him and his lovely family.

Fatima: Tell me about the type of business that you're currently doing.

Abe: My business is named Ramaka Solutions. Along with being a successful Amazon seller, I help entry-level to mid-level professionals who are stuck in an unsatisfactory corporate job to reinvigorate their passion through entrepreneurship.

I help people in the following circumstances:

- Working professionals at a crossroads in their careers who are deciding if continuing the rise up the corporate ladder is worthwhile for them. These people must inevitably make a decision – are they willing to continue sacrificing precious time to help large corporations get larger, or are they ready to take the plunge and invest time into their business endeavor. I advocate doing both at the same time.

- Working professionals whose personality does not mesh with the prototypical corporate leader. People who don't have a lot to say, and who don't say it the loudest, but quietly go about their work with little appreciation.

- Working professionals who are not integrated into the social hierarchy and who are not willing to rub shoulders with the corporate elite at the expense of their families and personal values.

- Working professionals who are fed up with working in a toxic environment where employee morale is suffering, high-level talent is lost, and there is little regard for work-life balance.

- Working professionals who are tired of seeing Managers who lack basic interpersonal skills get promoted and be given the authority to assess their Leadership acumen during performance reviews, despite lacking important Leadership attributes themselves.

- Working professionals who are tired of being micro-managed and of not being given the autonomy to make important decisions that will help them grow as Leaders.

- Working professionals who are tired of watching the red carpet get rolled out for executives and important visitors, while the efforts of front line Management are seldom recognized.

- Working professionals who are frustrated with the income ceiling that comes with years of stagnation in middle-management, and the fact that high performance does not equate to regular merit increases.

- Working professionals who know in their hearts that their corporate job is not satisfying their appetite for success and want more fulfillments from their careers.

- Working professionals who are determined to be successful and have the drive to make a difference in peoples' lives.

- Working professionals who enjoy new challenges and enjoy learning new skills.

So in a nutshell, I encourage people to discard the traditional 9-5 mentality that has been ingrained into their minds since early childhood. Most people consider all of the negative points I mentioned above to be standard norms in the workplace. That is not the case, and for me, the solution to all of these problems was entrepreneurship. I now have the power to make my own decisions and to right all the wrongs that I witnessed in the corporate world. I treat every single one of my customers and colleagues with the utmost dignity and respect, and I make them feel like they are the most important people in the world when dealing with my company. I make my own decisions based on logic and based on what's right for the customer instead of basing decisions on what showcases the best to the executive staff. I am the executive staff now – this is the mindset that I encourage the people I help to develop so they can escape the rat race and live the life they truly want.

F: From what I understand, you were frustrated in your workplace and you decided that you wanted to go into your own business. Is that it?

A: Yes, that's right. I was frustrated to the point where I was going to work every single day with a pit in my stomach for the last year and a half at my job. More than that, I was disappointed that a multi-billion dollar company that invested 12 years in my growth and development, did not realize how big these problems had become or that they even existed. This told me that the business was all about the bottom line and about protecting their chosen leaders, instead of being about the people that helped grow the organization into what it had become. This is when I decided to go into business for myself. Any workplace or business that does not have its people as the number one priority will ultimately destroy the morale and spirit of its workers. Most people are oblivious at first, and some choose to gut it out after this fact becomes obvious. It took me 12 years to realize this before I finally said enough is enough, and my goal is to reduce this timeline for people in similar situations.

F: Why did you decide to go into the Amazon business?

A: The world in 2016 looks nothing like the world of 20 years ago and there has never been a better time in history to build a profitable business with the evolution of the internet. My entrepreneurial journey began with a Facebook notification in February of 2015. I have always had the entrepreneurial spirit, but never before had I seen something that I felt in my heart that I could do on a full-time basis and enjoy doing it. The notification was in regards to becoming an Amazon seller, and knowing that we were in the midst of an ecommerce boom, I knew this was something that I would be motivated to do. I immediately began to take the necessary steps to become familiar with the process, and I signed up for specialized training to accelerate my development. The more I learned, the more I became hooked, and the thirstier I became for more knowledge. Within a few months, my business was off and running.

Another important factor in choosing to become an Amazon seller is that I was able to utilize 12 years of experience in the corporate world to my advantage. My professional background is specifically in manufacturing, engineering, and quality. The expertise I have in these areas, and my familiarity with the product development lifecycle, allow me to develop unique products that are based on what is referred to as the "voice of the customer". This means that I leverage customer feedback from other similar products to the one I am developing, and I build this into all of my products. This is a major differentiating factor between my brand and others, and a key component of my success. There is nothing more enjoyable to me than building a prototype, testing it out, optimizing it, and then settling on the final product. This is a lengthy process that most people are not willing to partake in, but an approach that I am happy to take knowing that few sellers play in this space.

Amazon allows me to develop high-quality products, to sell products that truly add value to peoples' lives, and it allows me the opportunity to interact with loyal customers to whom I can provide the highest level of customer service. Selling on Amazon allows me to have the flexibility to scale my business to any size I like with unlimited income potential. Finally, Amazon affords me the ability to interact with a network of like-minded individuals whose primary concern is to help others be successful and to achieve their goals.

F: Is this the first time in your life that you went into your own business or did you come from a family that had a business background?

A: I've dabbled in many ventures, but I never took anything seriously. Most of my past exposure to business was getting drawn into some get-rich-quick programs that I knew I would do nothing with, but signed up hoping that I could ride someone's coattails to riches. I think this is a big mistake a lot of people make, and why I love the Amazon model so much because you're buying and selling tangible assets that you have full creative control over.

The first business where I made a little bit of cash was when I started writing resumes for people. I love creative writing, and this skill served me very well when it came to writing resumes. I always did them for free for family and friends, so I decided to write an ad and post it online, and I got some business from it. One person paid me 400 dollars cash to write his resume, but most customers paid between 100 and 150 dollars. The problem with this business was that it took forever to effectively write a resume, especially when a customer worked in an unfamiliar field. So I stopped this completely, and my next real exposure to business was Amazon.

My mother is an entrepreneur herself. She was in her late teens when she came to Canada, went to beauty school, and then spent the first part of her career working for other people in hair salons. She then purchased her salon, before relocating into an addition she built onto our home. For the last 25 years, she's been blazing an entrepreneurial trail for me. She turned 60 last year, and she's still going strong. This motivates me to scale my business to a point where I can give her the gift of retirement!

My father is also an entrepreneur. He had a government job for 18 years before retiring to pursue his dream of being a successful online marketer. He has experienced his ups and downs, but what I admire the most about my dad is his laid-back approach to failure and how he lets nothing deter him from achieving his dreams. My father was a decade ahead of the current buzz of online businesses and is an example for the generation of immigrants in his age group. Now that I understand the opportunity presented to my generation in the digital world, I have much respect for my dad because he had the guts to leave the 9-5 lifestyle in hopes of achieving financial independence long before it was a common thing to do.

Entrepreneurship runs in my family! Watching my parents put the work in day in and day out inspires me to no end. None of them work in a corporate environment, and the politics I described earlier doesn't apply to them. My entrepreneurial drive was developed in part because I witnessed their extreme sacrifice. I can't imagine working that hard in my 60s if God prolongs my life, and I am going to do everything in my power to make sure I don't have to!

F: As you were working for this corporate organization and you were having these feelings inside you, was there some kind of a specific mindset shift? Did you need to change your thinking?

A: There was a monumental change in my mindset. I was one of those people who thought that the corporate environment was normal. Working 7 days a week, 12-14 hours a day, not getting paid overtime, having a tyrant for a manager, being forced to work "just because", missing special occasions with my family, changing my life schedule around to suit the needs of the organization, etc.. I thought this was the way it was, and it wasn't until I was introduced to the world of entrepreneurship that I realized that this was completely abnormal and that I had the power within me to create the life I wanted for myself and my family. To be honest, the more I learned about the Amazon opportunity and the doors that could potentially be opened for me, the more dejected I became about having to go to work in that environment every day. When I sat back and analyzed the situation, I realized that there was hope that I may get out of this mess, and that's when the shift in mindset took place. I needed to temporarily accept things as they were at my corporate job, knowing that it was a means to an absolute end. I decided I was going to get up and do my job every day because I needed to support my family, but I was going to rapidly accelerate the launch of my Amazon business and I wasn't going to let anything stand in my way. Psychologically, this changed everything for me – all the ills of the workplace became minor obstacles that I needed to clear while I focused on my business. Yes, it was still difficult to deal with some of these ills, but the positive energy that my Amazon business brought into my life far outweighed what I was going through at work. Knowing that the end was in sight and that I would have the last laugh made it easier to deal with my work situation.

F: You completely believed in the dream and that it would happen?

A: Yes, that is the most important thing. I believed whole-heartedly in the opportunity, and what I could do with it. You can tell how into something you are by the level of action you take. When I was learning the Amazon business, I 10xed my activity level. It was going to happen for me to come hell or high water. A typical day for me involved fulfilling my corporate job commitments, then fulfilling my family commitments, and then buckling down and working on establishing my business every evening until the early hours of the morning. I would then wake up bright and early and start the process all over again. This went on for several months until I established my business to the point where it was running on auto-pilot. It is true what they say about the power of positive thinking – I have never in my life felt so positive about something I was doing, and the results prove that the thoughts and energy you put into something have a bearing on the outcome.

F: So when you had this belief in you and you changed your mindset and your attitude, there was no stopping you?

A: There was no stopping me. If you believe in something, and you approach it with optimism and constant action, you are bound to be successful.

F: And there was no turning back for you?

A: There was no turning back. The goal was to press forward, establish a successful business, and then scale it as much as possible.

F: What is the most common obstacle that people who are in the corporate world go through when they're thinking about going into their own business?

A: The biggest obstacle for most people is time. There are only so many hours available every day with most time being gobbled up by the rigors of the workday, followed by endless family commitments. So people who are serious about starting their own business need to make a conscious decision to spend the majority of their spare time working towards its establishment. They've got to be willing to sacrifice some "me time" and sleep to build something special, which is exactly what I did.

I know most people have no qualms about spending three to four hours on Friday evening watching their favorite show or sporting event. Most people can't resist checking their Facebook notifications or email every other minute. People love to sleep in excess, hang out with friends, party, and partake in endless leisure activities in life, and this is normal. However, these things need to be scaled back in a big way if one is to launch a successful business in a short period. There is plenty of time available to become a serious entrepreneur if this is a priority in your life. You may alienate some friends in the short term, but in the process, you will learn who your true friends are. You may even end up being an inspirational force in your network of friends and may create some business partnerships as a result.

> Don't let (the lack of) time be the reason you accept mediocrity and fail to take action. Time is of the essence and as the saying goes, you must experience short term pain for long term gain.

My advice is to reduce the amount of non-valued added activity in your life as you get started, and the future benefits will be worth every sacrifice and then some.

F: How did you manage it? You've got your parents, you've got three beautiful children, you've got a wife, and you're supporting everyone financially. How did you do it?

A: Well, this required tremendous sacrifice on mine and my family's behalf. Before I began, I made sure my family knew how serious this journey was going to be and I obtained their buy-in. By involving them early and letting them know the time commitment required ahead of time, made the transition much smoother. All of my spare time was spent immersed in this business for the first 5-6 months, and it didn't get any easier after that because after the business is firmly established, an entrepreneur is always trying to scale and optimize.

There are some very practical steps one can take to help manage the chaos that comes with a business launch, particularly when it comes to managing professional and personal commitments. These 8 steps will help any entrepreneur optimize the time spent launching their business, while simultaneously igniting the motivational flame required for success.

- Do not go about this business where you completely isolate yourself from the world and neglect the priorities in life. The advice given above pertained to optimizing your time and spending less time on the less important things in life. You cannot become so fixated on this business that 100% of your time is devoted to it, and the people most important to you become secondary. This is a recipe for disaster, and a key measure of success is your ability to maintain balance in both areas. Do not use time as an excuse to neglect your family.

- Get your family and friends involved in what you are doing. Talk about your journey with them, ask for their opinion when it's called for, and show them the cool things you are learning, and have them participate in the various stages of business development. This makes the time issue irrelevant because now they will fully understand what you are doing while you are away from them. A very simple way that I involved my kids in my business was to use their initials as part of my business name, and I even had the kids integrated into my business logo design. They know that this business was built with them in mind, and if you ask them today what they want to do when they grow up, one of the things they will tell you is that they want to work for Ramaka Solutions. How cool is that!

- Multi-task and take advantage of precious "wait" times. For example, when I bring my children to their swim lessons or soccer practice, I will often have some business-related tasks that I can complete. Sometimes I'll plug in my laptop and get cracking, and other times I'll cue something up on my iPhone and use headphones to learn something and I'll take notes as I listen. I will often schedule an important telephone or Skype conversations during these times. The same applies to doctor's appointments, haircuts, and lunch breaks.

- Fill your mp3 player or phone with leadership and business material that can be played continuously every time you get into your car. This will help get you in the proper frame of mind and get you thinking like a successful business person. This will make you want to spend more time developing yourself and your business.

- Stay organized and have a task schedule to help keep you on track. For example, every 2 weeks I document my business income and expenses. Every week I review the keyword search results and sales conversions from my advertising campaigns on Amazon and adjust accordingly. Every month I create a new shipping plan with my supplier to ensure that

I don't run out of stock. Every day I review customer feedback and product reviews and I exchange dialogue directly with my customers. Planning time here will save you a lot of time down the road.

- Don't let the naysayers cause you to question what you are doing. Don't let negativity creep in where you are second-guessing yourself. Don't let a small incident with a loved one come between you and your dreams. You must maintain a worry-free mindset, and you can't spend any time dwelling on mistakes, or saying "I wish I had done…." When something goes wrong, analyze what went wrong, implement corrective actions to ensure it never happens again, and move on. A positive frame of mind alone will save you an unlimited amount of hours.

- Don't re-invent the wheel – find a person or process that has proven successful, and copy what they are doing. This is a major time-saver – avoid the pitfall of trying to do things on your own. Seek out the people who have successfully gone through the process you are embarking on, and ask them what they did and how they did it, then do the same thing. It's that simple and you don't need to waste time coming up with your solutions.

- Spend time giving back. When you achieve success, there is no doubt that you were helped along the way by certain people. So be sure to give to the next generation of entrepreneurs by offering your help and your expertise as they move along. I coach dozens of people for free through various Facebook communities, and I gladly share my spare time with aspiring Amazon sellers, just like people did for me. Another important aspect of giving back is to never forget to be thankful for the opportunities you have just to be able to do something that you love doing, let alone to make lots of money doing it. Remember those who are less fortunate than yourself, and be sure to always keep them in mind and to be generous as you accumulate wealth. Be charitable in the manner that works for you, and God willing it will be returned to you in abundance!

F: How can the readers find out more about you and if they want to contact you and just get more information about what you do?

A: The reader can find out more about my business by liking the Ramaka Solutions Facebook page. There's a lot of valuable content there and I am documenting aspects of my entrepreneurial journey which will whet your appetite for success. As I mentioned earlier, I am currently mentoring several friends and associates on a pro bono basis to help them achieve their goals and start living the life they want to live. Anybody who's going through some of the same struggles in the corporate world that I went through or anybody serious about starting their own business and becoming an Amazon seller can contact me directly. I can be reached through Facebook and Facebook Messenger by searching for Abe Arabi – I welcome any friend requests!

If anyone is interested in viewing and/or purchasing any of my Amazon products, they can visit my website at www.ramakasolutions.com or they can go directly to www.amazon.com (USA) or www.amazon.ca (Canada) and search for Ramaka Solutions. I am currently operating in the Amazon USA and Amazon Canada marketplaces.

F: Any final thoughts?

A: These are very exciting times so I encourage anybody with even the slightest entrepreneurial itch to jump in while the ecommerce ship is still at the dock because it won't be for much longer. Take advantage of the free resources available online, and make contact with anybody who is successfully playing in the space you are interested in. I encourage all readers of this book to harness this opportunity to become part of an unsaturated online business community, and to take action immediately to get your piece of the pie!

ABOUT THE AUTHOR

Abe Arabi is an automotive professional with over 13 years of experience specializing in vehicle manufacturing, quality management, quality control/ engineering, and process reliability. Abe holds a Bachelor of Applied Science degree in Mechanical Engineering, which he obtained from the University of Windsor, Ontario in 2003. Abe also holds a Bachelor of Science degree in General Science, also obtained from the University of Windsor in 1998.

Abe is the President and CEO of Ramaka Solutions, a company that he proudly founded in 2015 when he successfully fulfilled his lifelong aspiration of becoming an entrepreneur. Abe launched his ecommerce store on Amazon.com, designing and developing his brand of lunch bags that became Amazon Best Sellers in the process, and now generate a 6-figure income.

The success of Abe's Amazon business enabled him to walk away from a high-profile, rapidly progressing corporate career with a major automotive manufacturer. Abe left his 6 figure salary to focus his time and energy on expanding his business and now works for a small automotive company that has an entrepreneurial mindset and a management philosophy that is more congruent with Abe's beliefs and life priorities.

Abe lives in Windsor, Ontario with his wife and 3 children. Abe is actively engaged in the online Amazon community, helping dozens of aspiring entrepreneurs like himself build their Amazon businesses from the ground floor. Abe is currently working on the design and development of 2 brand new Amazon products that he hopes to launch by the end of 2016. Abe has recently expanded his lunch bag brand into the Canadian market, and will be launching in the United Kingdom in the summer of 2016!

Website
RamakaSolutions.com

Facebook
Facebook.com/RamakaSolutions

Email
info@ramakasolutions.com

Phone
1-888-463-3213

Amazon.com/Amazon.ca/Amazon.co.uk
Search"RamakaSolutions"

Notes:

HIND ADEAGBO

Stabilizing my health also really grounded me and played a fundamental role in me being able to think clearly and work on my mindset.

Fatima: Hind, tell us a little bit about your business. What kind of clients do you work with?

Hind: I work with Muslim women, particularly Muslim mothers in business. I help them heal and overcome challenges that have been keeping them from moving forward, and improve their energy and mindset so they can be more successful in their lives and businesses. I take a holistic approach where I look across how they are functioning in several areas of their lives and help them heal relationships, limiting beliefs and their health.

Many of the women I work with are coaches, birth workers, or health professionals who work in fields serving and caring for others. I help them bridge the gap and fill in the missing pieces where healing is needed in their lives. I think it's also really important that all of us build sustainable businesses, so we don't have to compromise our family, health, or values to make money and serve others. Most mothers want to prioritize their families and don't know how to run a business without it stealing time and energy away from what is most important.

F: What made you decide that you wanted to go into this field?

H: It has a lot to do with my personal story. I've run different businesses focused on women's health and success over the past 6 years. In the process of doing this, I experienced a range of challenges including the death of a child during birth, a crash to my health after my seventh child was born, the everyday struggles of balancing my family life while operating a business. My family has always been a priority to me and I didn't want my business to crowd out my family time.

I also discovered that my thinking could be quite negative and I had unresolved habits, emotions, and relationships that weren't benefitting me. Through the process of building my business, all of these issues came to the forefront, and I had to learn how to resolve them to keep moving forward. Eventually, I realized that if I was going through all of this other women must be too. I wanted to offer women a short-cut to their business success by supporting them to heal and resolve the issues in their lives that were holding them back.

F: What is the most common obstacle preventing women from achieving a successful business?

H: There are a few key obstacles that I see all the time. The first is time. What I see from mothers is that they have husbands, they have children, and sometimes they are also caring for elderly parents or in-laws or family members. They're wondering, how am I going to find the time to run a business? They don't know how to manage their time in such a way that they'll have room for more than what's currently going on in their lives. And of course, if they're going to do something, they want to succeed.

The second thing is confidence. Many sisters have dedicated their lives to raising children, which is very admirable, and now they're wondering if they can be of service and make some money from a particular skill. They have a lot of questions: "Do I have what it takes? Do I have enough training? Do I have the experience? Will I look professional?" Many mothers have a little toddler in the background who makes noise and you think "how is this going to work?" And then there's the unspoken looming fear that if you can make it work, it will change your family dynamic forever. That transition from stay-at-home mother to stay-at-home business mother can often feel daunting and impossible, leaving people frozen unable to move. This combination of lack of confidence and fear keep mothers stuck in the start-up phase, not taking action or stepping into the new role that awaits them.

The third obstacle, which kind of points to the first two, is the mindset. This is about women believing that this is possible and that there is a way forward even if they can't see it right now. Often due to our upbringing and life experience we have preconceived ideas or rules about what's possible and what's not. These beliefs colour how we interpret the world and interact with people. So if someone is not aware that there is a script running in their subconscious that is affecting how they think, and the decisions they make, they can become trapped in a false reality. Getting to know yourself, and how you think, makes it possible to determine that many of the rules you've made- up for yourself aren't true and give you the ability to break free from this false reality. The fact that you can free yourself is powerful and life-changing and gives you the foundation for business success.

The last big obstacle I see for mothers are unresolved health and relationship issues that steal from their energy, productivity, and focus. Our health is a trust from God and our bodies have rights over us. Ignoring aches, pains, headaches, fatigue, food intolerances, digestive issues, hair loss, tooth decay, or any other feeling or diagnosis won't rebuild your health or get you closer to accomplishing your goals. Time and time again I hear mothers talk about how they can't focus and when they sit down to work they feel overwhelmed. If their bodies are inflamed, their brains will also be inflamed and they won't be able to focus. We shouldn't be experiencing cognitive decline at 20, 30, or 40 and the fact that we are should be sending alarm bells. It's difficult to commit to raising a healthy family when you're lacking energy and not in top gear, let alone build a business.

Then there are relationship issues that many women keep quiet about that have a huge impact. If someone has a husband who is excessively controlling and harsh and is not connecting with them in a positive loving way, it's difficult to have the mind space to be creative. Or perhaps there are many past conflicts the couple has never been able to resolve that leaves the sister frustrated and heartbroken. When you feel like you're barely surviving on a day-to-day basis, it comes as no surprise that there's nothing left to give to your business, let alone yourself. Further, many mothers are battling with disconnected families and trouble with their young children and teens. Again, owning and running a business doesn't have much meaning to a mom whose family is falling apart. Your heart won't be there and rightly so. I've seen many mothers over the year leave their businesses to refocus on their family, but still not have the skills and resources needed to achieve this. Making the time and energy to commit to building your health and relationships can free women to focus on a more heart-centered businesses, and have success in their personal lives. So for business success, it's more about the woman you become in the process, and her becoming successful in all areas of her life than building the actual business itself.

F: What is the biggest pitfall that she is not even aware of?

H: What a good question! I think the biggest pitfall for women in business is prioritizing learning business skills over personal development and sorting out their lives. Most often the reason a woman isn't moving forward in her business are connected to mindset, being unaware of limiting beliefs, and not taking the time to resolve issues that are blocking her ultimate success. So I believe that if you're stuck anywhere in the business-building process you also need to check where you are out of alignment in other areas of your life, including your deen. There may be other more pressing issues for you to resolve. Your business has to fit into your life—instead of your life fitting around your business. I repeatedly see mothers who build their businesses quickly and with much more success after working to develop their mindset, build their health, and resolve family issues.

The second biggest pitfall I see is inconsistency. We all, want to prioritize our deen and families, which means as a mother we do have limited time when it comes to our businesses. What I say to moms is whatever time you have, use that time for your business and be consistent. Even if you're building it slowly and gradually, by continuous efforts, that's going to benefit you more in the long term than putting a lot of energy into something and completely dropping off for a week or two or a month before picking it back up again. So many mothers start and then when life gets busy they drop their businesses, and feel unmotivated to pick them back up again. That starting and stopping can paralyze your progress and burn you out quite quickly from those intense times of working on it without any focus and direction.

F: How do your clients avoid these problems while working with you?

H: I've created a holistic program that focuses on how women and mothers can be not only successful in their businesses but their lives and the hereafter. Once you heal yourself, the same strategies of success can be applied to any area of your life. I believe that especially as mothers, the first process of the start-up is figuring out how to make room in your life for your business so that you're able to work on the business consistently and become effective with time. Next is working on your mindset and what you believe is possible, what you believe is true. Then pulling back a layer and taking a look at yourself and your habits and how you show up in the world. What have you allowed for yourself and what have you not allowed for yourself?

Next would be evaluating your energy and rebuilding your mind and body so you can run a business and home productively. The last is looking at the close relationships in your life and evaluating how you are interacting and contributing—or not contributing—to a loving home environment. All of that processing is, I believe, foundational for starting your business. In my program what I do is spend that time, in the beginning, getting clear on all of this alongside your desires and goals, because I think as women and mothers we put ourselves aside. We've gotten lost in our day-to-day lives and become disconnected from our Lord. You are one person and how you do anything is how you do everything. So you can use the opportunity to build a business to become your best self and to come to your marriage, your family and your community whole and restored.

Throughout my program and definitely at the beginning we're asking "who are these women"? And who do you have to become to achieve your goals? So I would say if someone is looking for just marketing and get-rich-quick business building, my program wouldn't be appropriate for them.

However, if a woman is looking to improve herself, thereby creating a solution for more than one area of her life including business, then my program is for her. Again, because how you show up in one area of your life is how you'll show up in all areas of your life. If you're able then to support yourself in being the person who is going to run this business and run it successfully, that is the breakthrough.

> Creating the space for your business, prioritizing your personal development and resolving any outstanding issues will enable you to build your business quickly and successfully when you do learn the technical business building tools.

F: Most people don't even know that they are supposed to be looking for. How do you help them to understand how you do one thing is how you do everything?

H: I have a podcast, I run challenges, and I have courses where I address all of the issues, which helps women become more aware of the matters at hand. Awareness is always the first step. As a coach, working in groups or one to one, usually, people can connect the dots in our sessions.

I would guess if you've been trying to start a business and haven't been successful at it, meaning that you haven't actually gotten your business off the ground, or you've started your business and you haven't been able to make money from it, then there must be a missing link.

It's usually one of those areas that we're talking about, your relationships, including the relationships that you have with yourself, or maybe your health. By speaking to the lady and listening to what her struggles have been, we can start to see how we might fill-in these gaps together to help her get to where she wants to go. Even if sisters come aware of this, through our work together it becomes apparent to them what their obstacles are. This is part of the power of working with a coach. They can help you see life patterns and limiting beliefs that have been holding you back for most of your life. The sister herself must be open to seeing herself, dropping the old story, and do the work to become the woman she needs to be for the success she wants.

F: I read a Facebook status that said "he finds the result of achieving his success goals or his business goals, his relationships are suffering and he's come to the conclusion that it's inevitable." You can't have it all. You either are going to have your relationship or you're going to have your success. It's either one or the other. What would you say to a person like that who's made this kind of a decision?

H: I like the way you phrased it. You hit the nail on the head, to say to this mom that this is a decision. I think so much in life we experience is life happening to us and what we don't tend to experience is that we choose certain things and what we see around us represents a series of choices.

When you look at your life and what we experience on a day-to-day basis we have to understand that we all have free will, and with that free will we are making choices and decisions every day. We are responsible for those choices. We need to see the connection between the decisions we make and what's happening in our lives. If there is something positive that we want that would be good for us in our world, what harm could come from turning to God, and praying. We know all of our prayers are answered as believers, and trust God is always giving us what's best. So if we're running businesses as a way of clean income, or to care for our families, or contribute to building our communities, why wouldn't God help us to do that? Sometimes there may be a real need for a mother to share her gifts in a community or make money for herself and children, and if it's possible for one mother to do it successfully, it's possible for all.

It's our responsibility to fulfill all of our rights and obligations in our lives, so through prioritizing what God has commanded us to do, and intending good for our businesses - everything can work for us. If you allow yourself the possibility of something happening, then it can happen. If you close the door and you say to yourself "I can't" or "that's not going to happen" then it'll be very difficult for you to find a way to make that happen. Shift your perspective to know that with God's help, your intention, and the actions to go behind them, that anything is possible. Your job is to create the vision, pray, and take the steps. Then you rely on God for the results.

F: What did you do in your mind, your beliefs, to get here today?

H: I became a Muslim 21 years ago. That gave me a foundation for how I think, view the world, and the start of me being more optimistic as Islam is a religion of positivity and optimism. Also getting to know prophetic values and consciously allowing that to influence me. In more recent years there's been a journey for me in terms of becoming aware of the whole conversation around mindset and limiting beliefs. I wasn't aware that there was something called a mindset. That was important for me to know and the impact it had on me. When I started to learn more deeply about how my thoughts and beliefs influence my actions, my life was a game-changer for me. I was able to start putting the puzzle of my life together, seeing patterns I had established, and finally transforming things I'd wanted to change for years and didn't know-how. I always took my character and character development seriously and got upset if I did things I knew I shouldn't be doing. I was out of integrity with myself. So when I started learning about mindset and limiting beliefs it was a huge opening for me in personal transformation. It was like I had been given a key to open a door and to become everything I had always wanted.

Stabilizing my health also grounded me and played a fundamental role in me being able to think clearly. I was addicted to sugar most of my life and suffered from gut issues, which caused me to be irritable. So with the sugar gone, my moods stabilized, irritability waned, energy increased, and my focus skyrocketed. It was a huge weight lifted off my shoulders. I started reading daily and learning about the mind-strategies for success, changing habits, and how I could use all of my background, (the good and the bad), to help myself and not be a victim. It took me developing a mindset practice and consciously understanding that I had certain beliefs that were running the show, and letting go of those beliefs that were no longer serving me. I had to build a muscle around making new decisions, allowing myself to think differently, and understand that I get to choose what set of beliefs that I wanted to follow.

For example, I could choose to keep believing the story my subconscious mind was telling me about how I wasn't good enough to receive love in my life, or I could decide that story wasn't benefitting me or contributing to the kind of life I wanted to have. And this is sometimes not easy as we hold on to thoughts that harm us from our past because we're benefitting from it somehow. We can't change the past: what happened when we were little or what's happened in the past. We can change who we are and our life circumstances now. And each of us can create awareness and take those steps. These are all the outward steps I took, acknowledging the help from God.

It's a journey for me and not a destination.

F: Tell me Hind did you have the best, most awesome, God-conscious, transformational parents so that you could be the woman that you are today?

H: No one has a perfect life and I think sometimes we think that other people do and that's the reason for their success. Everyone has different pain points, struggles, and trials in their lives. That's the nature of the world. Someone can be going through a difficulty that we feel like is so big and might completely blow us out of the water and for that person, they're managing. God knows who can handle what and everyone has been given the circumstances God knows that they need to become their best selves. All of these situations that we find ourselves growing up in, have led us to the point that we are today.

My parents did the best they could, as every parent does the best they can. Anyone could choose to be critical and a victim, but that wouldn't change their circumstances. Everyone has the choice to see the countless blessings, advantages, and strengths our parents had and the opportunities they afforded us. I am certainly grateful to my parents for the values, love for learning, opportunities with education, and their desire to make me a well-rounded person.

How we experience the world is a choice. I was talking to a client today about creating joy for themselves and creating the experience they want to have in their life. We can't always change our circumstances but we can control our experience of it. Everything that God sends you in your life you can benefit from, and holding grudges and being bitter will only poison us. There's nothing that could happen in this world that could ever be a loss for us, except for the loss of our faith. If we are patient, there's a reward and if we are open there's a door for us to cross into something better. I would say a good portion of us have experienced something devastating, something heart-wrenching, something unimaginable in our lives, and it's for us to take that pain and use it to draw nearer to God and become better people, and servants.

I believe God gives us painful situations to become better, and for us to make better choices. We need to understand there is always more work to be done and we can always draw closer to God. Everything is an opportunity. Again it's about what experience you want to create for yourself and let that guide how you handle what's going on.

F: What rituals have you created as a mom, as a businesswoman, as a servant to God that propels you and creates success choices every day in your life?

H: Great question. As a mother I decided a long time ago that my responsibility to my family took priority over everything else in my life. I could serve God by changing a diaper, breastfeeding, cooking, or any other responsibility that fell under my household duties. That really saved me from feeling it was burdensome being a mother, helped me enjoy my family, and kept me in a positive mind-frame. It's important as mothers that we enjoy what we do, as our children are only young once and the years pass by so quickly. I made a point to understand that my whole life is worship, and if I intend drawing near to God with each act, it can lead me to success.

Sometimes I think mothers feel that they have to be engaged. Attending events, and be in the thick of things, so to speak, to make progress and feel spiritual, not realizing the blessing are in the very mundane activities they take for granted daily. I have six children, I had seven but I lost one as mentioned before. I had them back-to-back pretty much and my time, especially in those days, was mainly given to them. I had long hours. I chose that this is all worship and I continue to make that choice today. Developing a mindset that all of your actions are for the sake of God, including the time you spend with the women you serve, the time that you spend in your business, and the time you spend working on and developing yourself is, therefore, a key to success. If you try to keep this intention close to your heart it helps to keep you going. So putting your family first and fulfilling your obligations is a powerful means to have success in your business.

Reading daily and working on my mindset practice has also been really important habits. It has helped me stay in a frame of mind for expecting the best of myself and to keep growing. When I didn't take care of myself I ended up in a situation where I couldn't take care of them. It's been healthy for them to see that I am available to be a mother, for their companionship, to guide them and teach them, while also learning and growing myself. I also have strong boundaries with my business in the hours I work, the days and time I commit to. That means that I'm not at every mastermind or business event and when I do go, my kids understand it's a part of my development.

F: What is the best advice you would give to a woman that is considering launching a business?

H: Hmm… Goodness, what would I say? The best piece of advice? I would probably say evaluate first. So often we rush into things without thinking them through. I don't mean a long-drawn-out introspection where you stay stuck. I mean, however, that it's important to look at your life. Is your life set up right now for you to run a business?

Sometimes there's resistance for a reason. Sometimes you might feel uncomfortable putting yourself out there for a reason. Fear isn't always bad, it can be pointing us to something that needs to be addressed and may even have truth to it. Not everything is a mindset issue and there may be small or large things that need prioritizing in your life. There might be a reason that you're not set up for this right now. This doesn't mean that you can't start a business or you should stop working in your business. It does mean you need to dedicate time, and resources to support yourself.

Let's say you have an overwhelming health issue and you're not able to get out of bed. You don't have extra help, and you've got three kids at home. That situation cannot be ignored and you would need to evaluate your needs to be successful in your business despite these circumstances. It's not that you give up on the business dream, but you do what it takes to achieve success in your business. What I don't want to see is that you start a business without proper focus and a proper understanding of what it's going to take and end up frazzled or giving up.

I would also say work with people who are experienced with what you want to do. Don't recreate the wheel and fly solo. Most mothers in business end up hustling, don't have any strategy, and emulate others who also don't have a strategy. So while you are working on having your life in place, and upgrading your mindset and health, work with an expert in business and learn how to build a business instead of a side hustle. Setting up structures and systems is key to you being able to save time, streamline processes, and be more productive.

F: Thank you Hind. What's the best way for someone to get a hold of you and have a private conversation with you?

H: You're welcome Fatima. The best way to get a hold of me is to email me at hello@hindeadeagbo.com and connect. To learn about my work, the courses and coaching programs I offer please view my website http://www.hindadeagbo.com. I also run a free Facebook group specifically for mothers and high achieving women. In that group, I answer questions and often provide more detailed information through videos and posts. The Facebook group is called Mothers Making It Happen and I welcome anyone who is reading this to join our community online. I also work locally in my community. Email me if you live in my city or the UK and want to attend any live events or talks.

F: Any last-minute thoughts Hind?

H: What you are striving for is possible and can be done. Know that there are many other women in similar situations. So often mothers think we're the only ones in our particular situation. Maybe you're having a marriage problem right now or you're struggling with really valuing yourself and want to improve your confidence, or maybe you are struggling with parenting, or you feel burnt out and might have built up resentment. Whatever you're going through, know these are very common situations for mothers and you aren't alone. It is possible for you to overcome the situation that you're in, start your business and achieve whatever you want to achieve. Don't give up hope, and find a way to make it happen.

ABOUT THE AUTHOR

Hind Adeagbo is a transformational coach for mompreneurs who want to stop putting themselves at the bottom of the list. She helps them heal their bodies, replenish their relationships, and welcome love and abundance back into their lives.

A mother of six, Hind is a certified doula, childbirth educator, restorative exercise specialist, an IBCLC. She's also is a trainer of breastfeeding counselors and co-founder of a grassroots mother-to-mother breastfeeding support group.

After experiencing a devastating crash to her health after her last child, Hind retrained as an integrative nutritionist and functional diagnostic nutrition practitioner, transformed her diet and lifestyle, and grew a successful transformational coaching business.

Hind is passionate about helping mothers build optimal health, financial freedom and healthy lives at home so they can be successful in all areas of their lives. She has educated and supported hundreds of women in their childbearing years, helping them achieve their personal goals related to health, birth, mothering, and business.

Originally from Berkeley, California, Hind moved to the UK in 2002 after getting married. An aficionado of international travel and culture, she converted to Islam as a student in Cairo, Egypt in 1995, and later spent nine years living abroad with her family in Saudi Arabia.

Notes: ✍

Notes:

RIZWAN LOKHANDWALA

"Giving Back The Dignity and Pride To People"

Rizwan Lokhandwala took his money and invested in real estate. He understands what it's like to grow your money in a fast and incredible way. He surrounded himself with great mentors and now he manages rental properties for investors.

Fatima: Let's talk about your business. Please tell me a little bit about the kind of business you do and the kind of customers you have.

Rizwan: I own a property management company. It's called Onyx Real Estate Solutions and we manage rental properties for investors. If you're an investor and own rental properties, we offer integrated solutions that simplify dealing with the tenants, municipalities, and vendors. We collect rent, payout expenses, keep track of all the accounting, and complete maintenance requests. Essentially, we can streamline the entire process to maximize your returns with turnkey solutions. Whether you're in search of a new property, or the right tenant, we screen, execute leases, and manage the ongoing rental services. Most of our clients are professionals who work in a variety of fields that understand the importance of investing. They don't want to take on the time-sensitive tasks that can sometimes become overwhelming and they appreciate the efficiencies the right property management company can provide. The age of our investors varies, ranging from people in their late 20's into retirement. Whether you are just starting or have a great deal of experience, our company will be able to help in a variety of ways. We focus on mitigating risks to keep occupancy high, bad debt low, and maintenance low by evaluating and analyzing capital expenditures in the short term and long term.

F: Not everyone is into this kind of stuff. It's unusual. What led you to this field? Give us a little bit of a back-story.

R: It's weird. Ever since I was young, I have always looked at buildings and retail spaces and I would tell myself it would be amazing if I could own that and collect rent. I came up with the idea to invest in real estate in 2008 while I was in college at U of M - Dearborn. At the time, the university was a commuter college, and I found out they had plans to build dorms. I knew that the rental market near campus would be a great place to invest. Although I didn't have the funds to invest in these real estate opportunities at the time, as soon as I graduated, I dove into real estate.

With my dad's help, I bought my first rental property in February 2010. We bought it for $37,500 and last year I was offered $175,000 by a developer for that same property. So you can tell how deep the prices dipped for some of these single-family residential homes, and how much they came back up in 5 years. We were able to buy a few properties and I got into it. I gradually learned about the rehab and rental processes, though the learning curve was really big in the beginning. My uncle, who is a broker and has been in the business for over 25 years, really helped guide me in learning about what to look for before investing in a property. After about a year into it, he suggested that I start a property management company. I was managing my properties, so it made sense. I got my real estate license in 2011 and started my property management company with one or two clients. After that, it just started growing through referrals.

F: So the customers that you help are investors, right?

R: Yes.

F: What is the most common obstacle they have?

R: One of the most common mistakes I see people make before entering the real estate investment space is not having a well-thought-out exit strategy. In addition to that, for most investors, when you have one or two rental properties it becomes very hard to make relationships with vendors. If there's a maintenance request, a maintenance guy may not put you as a priority because you may only have one or two maintenance requests every three months. This might make it difficult for you to get things done on time. While the tenants get impatient and become unhappy, at the same time you may not have the leverage to negotiate the prices with your vendors with the low volume of work. With the number of houses I manage, I have been able to negotiate lower prices with my vendors for general maintenance, plumbing, HVAC, and legal services while getting maintenance requests done quickly.

I currently manage about 80 single-family rental properties. This creates a constant stream of business for my maintenance guy and some of the other vendors I use. Tenants and owners also have access to their online portals. Tenants can pay rent online at no cost to them or the owners and put in maintenance requests. Owners are also able to access monthly and annual reports showing the performance of their investment property and what expenses have been paid and which may be outstanding.

The owners never have to deal with the hassle of writing or depositing checks. They just get the rent that was collected that month minus the expenses. But, we also provide a more valuable service other than reducing expenses and eliminating hassles. We add value by letting our clients know where we feel the market is headed. We can better assess when it is a time to sell or a time to continue holding on to the property so we can maximize their returns. Being on the ground and driving the area from time to time, we can see changes in the neighbourhoods, which help us make changes in the exit strategies if the clients need to.

We also have better experience and understanding of where to make the right capital expenditures to minimize the expenses - long term and short term. For example, let's say there's a house that has constant issues with its driveway. Let's say the driveway may cost around $300 a year just to keep fixing, but it will damage the house until the driveway is completely redone. We can analyze and look at this and tell the client that spending $5,000 today to redo the entire driveway may be better in the long term. The damage to the house could create a repair expense far greater than $5,000 in the future. A new driveway would eliminate the yearly expense of $300, increase the value of your home, and you may be able to get a greater pool of applicants.

With a bigger pool of tenants, you're able to minimize your risk of having a bad tenant coming in or us having to evict them in the future. Not only do we provide the management services and deal with the day-to-day operations, but we also provide free consulting along the way to analyze their investment and its profitability and sustainability.

F: A lot of Muslims come from a middle-class mindset. Did you have to change your mindset, your attitudes or your belief systems for you to come at this point? Or was it very natural for you to say I am not going to get a job after university?

R: The property management company started on the side but I've always had an entrepreneurial mindset probably from the beginning. Even in high school, I had to write an essay about what I wanted to do in the future to get accepted and oddly enough I wrote an essay about how I wanted to start an investment company, pool money together from different investors, and help them invest it. I have done exactly that. Although today we're talking about my property management company, I also run three real estate investment companies that follow a similar business model.

I've been able to help individual investors who may not have been able to invest in real estate on their own, invest in real estate on a larger scale. By pooling smaller investments with more investors, I have helped them minimize their risks and created an opportunity for a greater compounding growth effect. As far as me not wanting to get a job, I don't think I had to transition or change my mindset. Even in college, I was doing different types of businesses. I didn't look for the intern positions or anything like that. I started a marketing company, I was into sales, and I was doing a variety of different things where I was dealing with small businesses and different types of clients. So I guess I've always really had an entrepreneurial mindset.

F: How did your family react when you didn't get a job after University? Are they also entrepreneurs?

R: My dad came to the U.S and went to college and studied to be an engineer. While he was studying, he ran a few businesses and even when he was an engineer he always had a business on the side. Now, he's a retired engineer from Ford but currently owns a financial advising company. So I think in our family we have always been into business. My mom has been a stay at home mom. Both my parents have always supported me in whatever I wanted to do, although when my business wasn't as big as it is now, they would be concerned as any normal parent would be. What I realized is anything that I do and in any business that I try and start, the only ones I am successful in are the ones that I persistently continue to work at. Real estate was something that I have never stopped working. My mind is always on it. Once you have that focus, it is easy to keep moving forward.

F: A lot of successful people talk about rituals and habits. Do you have any specific habits and rituals that you do that's an indicator of your success?

R: As far as I know, I don't have any specific habits. But for me to be able to do or get any work done, everything has to be organized. I would say I am a very organized person. I get up in the morning, I make my bed, I know what I have to do, where I am going to start and I just start doing it. When you are doing what you want to do and you don't look at the time, and when you are focused, you don't even think about breaks sometimes to even eat. If I have to work after normal business hours, it doesn't phase me. Whether I have to meet a tenant or go meet a client, I do it; the time does not matter as long as I don't have anything else planned or scheduled.

One of the main positive feedback I get from my clients is that they don't have to worry about a lack of transparency or any type of dishonest or unethical conduct with me. Some of my clients have dealt with dishonest property management companies that may overcharge for services, receive kickbacks from vendors, or take short cuts in repair jobs which may end up costing the client more in the long run. When you conduct business most honestly and transparently possible, your business will have the potential for exponential growth. That's probably the best advice I can give someone in starting any type of business. I have been in the property management business since late 2011. I still until this day do not have business cards, but I have gotten some excellent referrals from my clients. I have made plenty of mistakes over the years, and in some instances, I ate up a lot of the costs for some of the clients. A client or customer would rather you own up to your mistake and tell them how you plan to rectify the current situation, and how you plan to prevent the situation from occurring in the future, rather than you trying to hide the mistake or pass the blame on to some other condition or person. I would say this is probably one of the indicators of my success.

Before starting any business, you see if there is a market for the product or service you're providing, and look at the opportunity and the ability for you to seize that opportunity, but after that, I try to see what I can do differently from the competitors. You just have to keep moving forward. My focus is not a foundation based on money, and though the bottom line is important, for me it's more about how much more I can do and how much better can I do it. I think that's a big differentiating factor when you are motivated to create the best product or service rather than trying to make the quickest dollar. Your business has a better ability to thrive.

F: What advice would you give a young person who's come from a middle-class family whose parents have never gone into business? They want to do either what you do property management and invest in real-estate or they want to tap into their passion but they don't know-how. What would be the first thing they should do?

R: Whatever you are passionate about, I suggest working towards it. You have to look at the opportunities in front of you and analyze your point of entry into that field. If it is real estate, you may start in sales, working for a company as a property manager, or maybe in construction, etc. Wherever you start, make sure you are learning from it. The most important thing is that you are learning something that will help you achieve your end goal. You also have to not be afraid to take risks. You may fail at numerous attempts, but it will all be worth it for the attempts you succeed at.

Though I love real estate, I have bigger goals than just trying to get ahead in that field. When I talk about bigger goals, I mean what I am planning to do to make an impact in this world. You have to figure that out on your own, but I think it's very important to do this. Whether it is to help people who may need proper housing, clothing, food and water, attention to their mental and physical health, or something like building a place of worship or rebuilding a park, etc.

You can be in any field and have goals or ideas of how you plan to make this world a better place. Figure this out and tie-in whatever businesses you start or career you enter into with a plan to progress your vision.

F: Thank you. What happens in your day-to-day? What drives you? What's that fire inside you?

R: I don't know if you've ever been to the city of Detroit. You can find common economic differences of any metropolitan area in any part of the world, but the defining red lines are very apparent in Metro Detroit. You start to wonder why some of the most expensive real estate in Michigan may sit just north of a particular road, but one of the faster-deteriorating cites in Michigan lies just south of that road, maybe not even more than two miles away from the prospering city. You ask yourself, what is the cause of this? Is it the way the city is managed, is it the culture of the people living in the city, is it due to the lack of resources or lack of planning? Growing up in the metro Detroit area, I have always wondered what the main underlying causes of the diminishing middle class are, and how we can find a solution.

I think those are the thoughts that drove me to look at real estate differently, and I think my constant curiosity in trying to answer some of these questions keeps me attached to it. When I first got into it, I wanted to buy out blocks of Detroit and redevelop them into proper housing for lower-income families. In my experiences, I have learned numerous factors may affect the sustainability of a project like that. The economics and the cycles of real estate may be a bit more complicated, and I think continuing to learn and trying to find a real sustainable solution for these kinds of projects is what drives me to dive deeper into the real estate field.

F: It's important for you to make housing better for people?

R: Yes, it is one of the things that I think about. I don't want to be a slumlord, and I am not. When I fix up and rehab these houses, I like to take pride in their present ability. When tenants move into a house, I want them to take care of it and their neighbourhood. I want people to just enjoy and appreciate where they live. I want to help them feel and learn that they make a big difference in helping to create a better community. I think if I can help make housing a bit more comfortable for a family, maybe they can focus on other things that can help them get further ahead in life.

F: If someone wants to connect with you and find out more information about your company to help them with property management, what would be the best way?

R: Well they can go to my website www.onyxres.com. My contact info is there. If they want to send me an email or call me I'd be more than happy to respond to any questions. Not only do I provide property management services, but I also provide consulting services if someone wants to invest in real estate on their own. I encourage everyone to spend some time and learn about real estate, especially if they don't have any experience in the field. It can teach you a lot about the world and broaden your view.

ABOUT THE AUTHOR

I am a high performer that strives to bring innovation, leadership, and value to his team. I have collaborated with numerous associates in cross-functional fields to meet and exceed expectations and continuously complete projects on time and within budget. I have worked on gathering requirements, design & planning, and implementing projects with SMEs, Developers, and Business Partners to successfully drive results for my clients. I graduated from U of M –  Dearborn with a BBA in Finance & Accounting and have gained over five years of professional and entrepreneurial experience while developing effective task management, computer, and communication skills. I am strongly equipped to enter into a career that values technical acumen, deep business training, career growth, and allows me to make a lasting impact on the company as a whole.

Website
Onyxres.com

Email
RL@onyxres.com

Work Phone
248.675.5259

Fax
248.284.4110

Instagram
Naaksaafkur (personal)
Rizeats (food)

Snapchat
RizWon

Twitter
RizWon

Notes: ✍

Notes: ✍

ARUN SARSAWAT

"Building 8-Figure Business"

No matter where you are in business, Arun Saraswat can take you and your company to 7 figures and more. The co-founder of The Muslim Mastermind is a mentor for entrepreneurs who want to launch Amazon businesses and get their mind designed for success.

Conversation with Arun Saraswat

Fatima: Tell me about your business and the types of customers that you help.

Arun: What I am going to discuss today is Mind Propel. I've been in business and entrepreneurship for about 15 years. The combination of that experience through software, technology, real estate, investing and digital marketing is the mixture of the business Mind Propel. The primary audience that we're looking to help are business professionals. Those who are in a professional setting or an entrepreneur who wants to learn the techniques, mindset or actual hard skills that are necessary to grow and expand their business.

F: What do you do for your clients?

A: I think everybody is in business to achieve certain goals.

1. First, identifying what those goals are.

2. Clarifying those goals.

3. And giving people a purpose

Whether its entrepreneurship or working for themselves, everybody wants to achieve certain things. So we help people clarify what that is, why are they working and what they want to achieve. Once they get clarity on that object we can outline a course of action for them. That action can include learning particular things and implementing those in their lives. For us, I have several associates with me in this business and we've been through so many lines of businesses and years of experience, we can help guide the professionals and business people that come to Mind Propel for help.

F: Having so much in your background and doing a lot of things, how did you get to say, "I'm going to bring all of this and focus it into one thing"? What was the switch?

A: We've been through so many different kinds of businesses from start-ups, solopreneurs, to Fortune 500 large contracting companies like IBM, Canon, and Mark-It Market. I've been in the public sector and the private sector.

I can relate to most people out there. There's a common set of 8 or 10 principles that govern how to increase the effectiveness, efficiency, output, and growth of any type of industry. They are common across the board. I've been able to see that across so many industries, and we can leverage it for anyone out there.

F: What do you think is the most common obstacle preventing the reader from actually achieving that kind of success they're hungry for?

A: The number one thing that I have seen in others is I would call "under an umbrella mindset". It's going down to a definition of what that is because it's a broad term. It is used in different contexts depending on who's using it and what context you are using it in.

The mindset, in general, is a set of thoughts and ideas that someone carries in regards to life in general and their business specifically.

A quick example of something we would work on with a mindset issue and where mindset can become a problem is somebody understands of what they are capable of doing. Many times a business owner or a professional will put a limit on themselves. May be in terms of revenue or salary people think six figures is somehow an arbitrary mindset limitation. If I could just achieve six figures I would be happy but that's an arbitrary number.

Six figures or seven figures. The difference between 100,000 and a million isn't that big of a deal. It's just getting over that in your mind. Once we get over that, it is simply putting a plan into place to achieve that number.

First, if I were using an umbrella term, I'd call it mindset. There are a lot of things. It may be limiting beliefs around the concept of money.

Unfortunately, many people have this idea that money is evil. There's a guilt associated with being wealthy or well off. People absorb those ideas and things in various ways. What I have seen for most people the first thing and the primary thing that becomes an obstacle to their growth is the way that they think about things.

F: What can a person do to overcome negative beliefs and mindset?

A: In terms of their mindsets, the only thing that can overcome somebody's mindset is to be constantly in the presence of other ideas that are challenging their current status quo. That could be found through reading materials, online videos, YouTube or being around a network of successful people.

For example, if I were somebody with a set of limiting beliefs around my earning potential, I would seek out people who earn at least 10x of what I do and talk to them. I would talk to them about my belief and why I only believe I can make $100,000 a year.

I would go to people who make a million a year and ask, "How did you get here?" and challenge your status quo of beliefs and ideas. I think that's the only way you're going to grow mentally. That's the first step. There are many steps after that but the first thing for the reader to understand. If you have a set of (negative) beliefs then you have to test the veracity of those beliefs. You have to talk to people that are operating at a different level than you. Put it into the context of business, earnings, and obstacles.

Read books by people who are surpassing you. And those who are not holding on to the same belief as you.

You have to test your ideas in the realm of the various ideas that exist out there. Once you expose yourself more to the people that carry a different set of ideas, the stronger the ideas hold and you start adopting those new ideas through a very natural process. Your brain is going to have some sort of cognitive dissonance where you are constantly exposed to and that tells you that XYZ is possible and you are carrying a set of ideas that say XYZ is not possible. The more you are exposed to those ideas and the more you understand that it is, it's a very natural process to start adopting the real ideas.

F: Were you born in a family where everybody was always questioning beliefs and limits. What happened for to change your mindset?

A: It was not normal. Most people are programmed. I guess it's very natural for people to have a set of beliefs and be comfortable with that. When those beliefs are challenged, it's not a comfortable feeling at first. As we mature, we want to know or seek the truth. That's easier for some people vs. others. I think I was okay with that at a very young age for various reasons.

What usually happens is you'll get challenged or be presented with something that challenges your set of beliefs. You either choose to ignore it or kind of lean on it. There are sets of people who are curious and they lean into it and there are a set of people who ignore and avoid it. You're going to fall in one of those two camps. My advice to people is to lean into, get used to discomfort because that's a process and that's a crucible. You're going to put your ideas in this crucible and it gets heated up and you'll go through a period of discomfort. But at the end of it, you'll get rid of a lot of impurities, which we call untruths or falsehoods.

You'll be left with a set of beliefs that relates to God in a larger context and the goals of human life.

What set of business beliefs or a belief about provisions and earnings that are going to remain pure and align with what reality that presents itself? So that's something I was comfortable with at a young age. I was okay with discomfort. I was okay with challenges.

F: It seems like you become comfortable with being uncomfortable.

A: Yes and that also helps a lot in business.

F: What are some of your rituals and habits that you have created that propelled you to success and attracted you to successful people?

A: I would say that's probably one of my weakest points, creations of habits that I consistently stick to.

The largest factor for me in terms of habitual practice that I have engaged in for at least 3-4 years, is building my network. I made a very conscious effort about 4 years ago to seek out people who I wanted to be around me. People who I could benefit from and very consciously grow the network of close friends and associates that I have. I have been able to very consistently do that week after week, month after month, growing that network and building personal relationships with people. I think a lot of people have different strengths and weaknesses and that's something I am always working on.

In today's society, it's very difficult, with all the distractions, devices, and communication methods, to engage in very consistent habits. That's a big challenge for a lot of people, entrepreneurs and professionals, parents, kids, everybody. It's hard to build sustainable habits that you stay consistent on but for me, one area of strength that I have is to consistently build my network and I've been able to do that almost every month. I reach out to new sets of people, building relationships, talking about areas of collaboration, and ideas on how to grow. That's been very consistent.

F: What advice would you give to the readers coming from a middle-class mindset?

A: Your tradition already gives you the raw material and the inspiration that we need to succeed in life. First, look at the life of The Prophet Mohammed (PBUH). He is specifically the greatest creation that ever walked the earth. His life is a living example of what it means to be successful in every area of life. The most important thing that I take away from his life and in general, Muslims should kind of adhere to be that prophet who lived on a set of principles and those principles are grounded in the religion of Islam. They came from the Holy Book and as that Muslim Leader said he is a walking Holy Book.

He embodies those principles and the entire concepts that are relayed in the Holy Book directly from God, the embodiment of that living, walking, and breathing. Understand that relationship. Once we understand that relationship what we see is that his actions, daily actions as mundane as cooking food or being with his wives and children, sewing his clothes, cleaning the house, the very mundane actions that we can all relate to, to the very grandiose actions of forming a state, meeting a people, uniting different pluralistic societies in Medina, growing an empire, talking to kings.

From the mundane to grandiose, it was all governed by those principles. He never violated those principles. Ultimately, the Muslim aims to live that principle lifestyle when it comes to understanding what their purpose is.

For me, as a Muslim when it comes to the context of business and growth and things like that it's to never violate those principles. Understand what are the principles that Islam have around this area of business growth and income and when it comes to commerce and money and provisions and take those principles and enact them and adhere to it as you live your life essentially.

F: If the reader thinks that they might be ready to connect with you and they want to find out more information about the Mind Propel, what is the best way for them to connect with you?

A: They can hop on the website www.mindpropel.com or they can reach me on Facebook Arun Saraswat. I'm pretty active there.

Just another piece of advice, you might want to pick one or two platforms and grow your presence. There are several social media platforms but I primarily use it for personal communication and business and I think Facebook to me is probably the greatest market tool ever invented in humanity. That's where I put most of my effort and presence.

If the reader wants to kind of think about how they want to get their message across to the world or connect and network, pick a network. Whether it's LinkedIn, Facebook, Snapchat, Twitter, or whatever it is and takes some effort to grow in that particular social media channel. To me, it's returned multiple times in the ROI.

Mind Propel is not limited to the Muslim space although everybody pretty much that works here is Muslim and we adhere to the Islamic principles. We are not overtly serving the Muslim community as such. Whereas the Muslim Master Mind is very particularly focused on helping the Muslim community. A lot of the influence for that came from me attending various marketing events for the past 4 or 5 years. I've invested over $100,000 in my education and while attending these types of seminars, I saw a lack of Muslim participation. A lot of my business growth can be attributed to the network, techniques, and strategies that I learned in those forums and settings.

F: How do you create balance of being a husband, a brother-in-law, son-in-law, son, father, and businessman?

A: That's a challenge. A challenge to anybody who wants to achieve anything in life. Balance is an area of compromise. I think at a certain time in your life you are focused on various things and that's what you focus on. I don't believe I'm so focused on business growth at the moment. It is a major area of my life but there are one or two other areas that include a family that is a bigger area of focus. If I were to put that on the side, I would grow exponentially larger in terms of the business and financial stuff. That's not the number one priority at the moment. I don't want to say it's a myth but necessarily balance is achieved through compromise. I don't think anybody can function at 100% in every area of life.

If you outline areas of life, typically people have 6 or 7 areas of life that include spirituality or religion, community, family, self-development, career/finances or business, and one or two others' health and that kind of thing.

At any time in anyone's life, you are going to be functioning at very high levels on two or three of those and you're going to be compromising on another few of those. That's okay. You have to understand what your capacity is. People function at different capacities, to understand that you can't ignore anyone and you have to have a plan balancing that out at some point and stick to it.

I think a lot of times people lie to themselves as well. They say "I have everything balanced".

Whereas, if they did a proper audit of what's happening you have to be truthful. You have to understand what the truth is. For people who are on the road 20-25 days out of the month, I would challenge to say that they're balanced with their family. I don't think you are. That's just the truth.

There may be a whole years where you focus on certain things. That's an individual call that you have to make and compromise with your family together and also with your community and society in general. I have a little bit of a different take on the balance thing. I don't proclaim that I'm super balanced. I let some areas go and focus on other areas. It's not a permanent thing. It's a conscious thing to be focused at this particular time for this amount of time and then to be honest with one's self. When that time is over, switch over to make sure other areas are addressed. I think that's the very normal and natural way to proceed if you're not lying to yourself too much.

ABOUT THE AUTHOR

Arun Saraswat brings over 15 years of technology consulting, start-up and executive experience to Mind Propel. Formerly he served as VP of Bayyinah LLC, where his growth hacked the company to over 10X results across multiple metrics. Annual revenue grew from 6 figures to 8, employees went from 4 to 45, departments increased from 2 to 8 and social media reach grew to millions - within 24 months.  He also helped grow the largest (to date) Islamic Video on Demand platform (Bayyinah TV) to over 50,000 subscribers. Before Bayyinah, Arun worked on a variety of commercial and federal software development and mobile projects in collaboration with companies such as IBM, Canon USA, Mercedes Benz USA, and many more. Arun has also played a founding role in education, technology, and real estate investment start-ups.

He can be reached at Mindpropel.com and EcommGoldrush.com

Notes: ✎

FARHAN MALIK

"Leaving a Legacy"

Farhan Malik loves the quote by Thomas Edison "I haven't failed 10,000 times. I've found 10,000 ways that didn't work". He educates people to invest their money in real estate.

Conversation with Farhan Malik

Fatima: Please tell me about your business and the types of customers that you help.

Farhan: We are in the real estate industry. Executive Realty Solutions is a private real estate firm that focuses on helping sellers, buyers, and investors. We purchase properties from sellers who need to sell quickly. These individuals may be facing foreclosure or have an unwanted property they can no longer keep up with. We help them get out of debt and move on to the next chapter in their lives. The properties we purchase usually need renovations, and ultimately we provide modern and updated properties to buyers looking for a home. We also work with investors who are looking to put their hard-earned money to work for great returns without interest. These investments are paid out through equity and profit split business model, which avoids interest completely. For investors who want to build long term wealth and financial stability, we connect them with cash flowing income properties. Finally, for those who want to learn the business and actively source deals, we provide training and mentorship through our real estate educational company, Thinkademy.

We have trained and mentored over 100 students and have successfully helped our students close deals in multiple states.

Fatima: What led you to this field? Is this what you always wanted to do when you were going through high school and college?

Farhan: In high school, I was originally planning on studying computer engineering. However in my senior year, serendipitously, I registered for an entrepreneurial class that I needed to fill my elective requirements. I instantly fell in love with the subject and knew that this was my passion. I decided to enter a competition hosted by DECA in which students had to come up with a new business idea, create a business plan, and present in front of judges. I ended up placing second in the state of NJ and advancing to the national championship competition in California. The entrepreneurial class and competition completely shifted my mindset and I knew before entering college that I wanted to get into business for myself and build a legacy. My passion and will to build a business grew stronger during my last year in college while I was interning for Johnson & Johnson. The bureaucracy, micromanagement, and office politics pushed me away from wanting to build a career in Corporate America and closer to becoming an Entrepreneur. At the end of the workday, I felt apathetic towards my job and felt that I was not building anything that got me closer to fulfilling my purpose and goals. I immediately started taking action to change my course in life. To my parent's disappointment, I changed my engineering major to economics and business. I also started seeking knowledge and connecting with likeminded individuals. I became friends with another student who had his Realtor license and immediately enrolled to get my Realtor license.

I trained under Mohammad Abbasi, the regional franchisee owner for Keller Williams. I also picked up as many books on real estate and business that I could get my hands on. Rich Dad, Poor Dad by Robert Kiyosaki gave me a new perspective on business and my formal education at Rutgers. I knew that my formal education would groom me to become a good worker, but would not teach me the financial and entrepreneurial skills I needed to build something of my own. It was at this moment that I knew I wanted to become an entrepreneur and focus on real estate.

Fatima: As you look at some of the clients that you've worked with, what do you think is the biggest misconception about real estate investing in the U.S?

Farhan: People are afraid to get started with real estate investing. The primary fear is the lack of money to invest. This fear stems from a lack of real estate education. Real estate is a vast industry and if you know how to market yourself, source deals, and find cash buyers, there are many ways new investors can structure deals without having to come out of pocket.

Fatima: And what can those people do to overcome those obstacles?

Farhan: The first step is to seek knowledge. Once you start learning, the strategies will begin to make sense. Once you implement those strategies, the deals will come and opportunities to the joint venture, tap into retirement accounts, and use creative financing will become apparent.

Fatima: Is this kind of investing that you're talking about and the people that you help, solely people who live in the USA?

Farhan: People from different parts of the world have attended our seminars, but most of the engagement from outside the U.S. has been through our online videos and posts. We see a tremendous opportunity to share knowledge and real estate techniques that transcend our local market and can be applied to countries outside of the U.S.

Fatima: Were you always like this? Were you raised with a family that was open-minded and entrepreneurial-minded where they encouraged you as a child to go into this kind of self-development or was this a transformation that happened to you?

Farhan: We come from modest means. My dad is a chemist and my mom was an office administrator for a medical office so the entrepreneurial spirit was not ingrained in me. I was not fed with a silver spoon and did not have opportunities to take over a family business. This motivated me to work hard. Even as a kid, I would try to barter and trade. When new video games would come out, I would hustle and sell my outdated games to save up enough money to purchase the new games. Commerce was in my blood and as I got older I was certain that I wanted to take the path less traveled by foregoing the corporate job and going into business for myself.

Fatima: Let's talk a little bit about failure. How has failure, pain and the challenges helped you to grow and be the person that you are today?

Farhan: Thomas Edison says, "I have not failed. I've just found 10,000 ways that won't work." You have to understand that success is never a straight line. There are turns, ups, downs and squiggly lines along the way. These detours on the path to success are not failures; they are lessons. These learning lessons are necessary for you to understand what doesn't work and make the necessary adjustments to succeed. The only way you stop learning and fail is when you quit. In my case, there have been many deals that have not gone well, but persevering and being able to go back to the drawing board has always allowed me to progress.

Fatima: If you had a few minutes, what would you say to the younger Farhan, age 19?

Farhan: I would tell my younger self to start seeking as much knowledge as possible and to never let fear get in the way. I would tell my younger self that life is not all about money. It's important to take care of yourself and your family from the fruits of your hard work, but it's imperative to remember there is a higher obligation. There is an enormous responsibility that is bestowed upon those who are given wealth by God to use the wealth, influence, and resources to help those who are in need. I would tell the younger version of myself that our time in this world is limited. Focus on building a business that leaves behind a legacy long after you are gone. Everything ultimately belongs to God and will return to God. You want to make the most of your time here and do the most good that you possibly can.

Fatima: Give us a little glimpse of what habits and rituals you do that have made you the man that you are today?

Farhan: The one habit that has helped propel me to the person I am today is waking up early in the morning. I recommend reading The Morning Miracle. Every day I wake up about an hour before Fajr prayer so I can review my mission statement, visualize my dreams, track my goals, and exercise. Reviewing my goals daily, praying, exercising, and reciting affirmations early in the morning gives me the confidence to take on anything that may come my way during the day. When your mornings are setup the right way it leads to productive days, which leads to productive weeks, which leads to productive years, which then ultimately leads to a productive life.

Fatima: What would be the best piece of advice that you would give someone that's considering working with you, investing in real estate or want to join your team?

Farhan: I would tell anyone that is looking to get started in real estate to seek knowledge and take action. Most people that I see who are not successful in real estate get paralysis from analysis. Knowledge is of no use without action. Seek knowledge and then look to apply and implement that knowledge immediately by taking massive action.

Fatima: If somebody wants to get hold of you and work with you, what's the best way for them to connect? Do you have a Facebook page? A website?

Farhan: Anyone looking to learn more about real estate investing and details on our upcoming events and classes can head towww.thinkademy.net. There's also a ton of free real estate tips that can be found on our video blog atwww.thinkademy.net/blog. For those who are looking to invest with us and for those looking to purchase turnkey income properties, they can visit our websitewww.execrealtysolutions.com. You can also connect with me on Facebook at www.Facebook.com/FarhanMalik01

Fatima: Any last-minute thoughts?

Farhan: Real estate investing is not very difficult and it is very possible to become successful in this industry. Real estate has created more millionaires than any other industry. Get educated, take action, learn your markets, and understand your appetite for risk. If you get a really good handle on these things, evaluating deals will come naturally. Then focus on branding yourself and marketing. Once you learn how to market for deals, raise funds, and find buyers, you will be well on your way to building an enormous business and focusing on creating your legacy.

ABOUT THE AUTHOR

Farhan Malik has been an Entrepreneur and Real Estate Investor for over 10 years. His private Real Estate Firm, Executive Realty Solutions based out of Somerset, NJ, focuses on acquiring distress properties, renovations, and selling at market value. In the process, the firm helps homeowners sell quickly and avoid foreclosure, keeps contractors and real estate professionals employed, and helps homeowners fulfill their dreams of  homeownership. The company also helps investors by connecting them with rental properties that offer double-digit returns and fix and flip deals that are based on equity and profits rather than loans and interest.

Farhan Malik has also been educating other investors and the general public on real estate and how to get started. His company, Thinkademy offers live courses covering Rehabs, Rentals, Wholesales, Marketing, and Raising Capital. He offers free videos on the Thinkademy blog and the Thinkademy team is busy building an online portfolio of Real Estate and Business videos.

Executive Realty Solutions Website
ExecRealtySolutions.com

Investors looking to invest passively
ExecRealtySolutions.com/investors/

Investors looking to get into the business
Thinkademy.net

Blog
Thinkademy.net/Blog

Notes:

FARID KHAN

"Digital Marketer & Mobile App Distributor"

Farid Khan is an expert digital marketer. He knows exactly how you take a mobile app, advertise it, monetize it and make it into a success. He's the CEO of Infinitely LLC and Muslimdigitalmarketers.com. He helps people understand the digital world and how you can make sense out of it.

Conversation with Farid Khan

Fatima: Please tell me about your business and the types of customers that you help.

Farid: I own a couple of companies. One of them is called Infinitely LLC which is my corporation in Melville, New York and I have another company which is called App Two.

Infinitely is my company where I run most of my professional services and business through my IT services. But what I do most of my work in mobile marketing is AppTwo. What I do there is help developers who just made an app or just built an app or went through all the basics of building an app and put it online, put it on iTunes or Google Play, but they're not getting the number of installs.

They are not getting as many organic installs as they would like to have. What I do is a couple of things. We give the developer a full scale projected plan, a solution for their app distribution. We go anywhere from simple app distribution where the user may just want 100 to 200 installs a day, all the way up to thousands of installs per day. That's one side of the business, directly with the developers who want their app distributed.

On the other side, we also do affiliate marketing, which again is app distribution. So these other bigger corporations or bigger entities like King Digital, Electronic Arts, Activision Blizzard, Dina or Machine Zone to name a few that have these games or apps and they are looking for other publishers to distribute the app. So, we do those kinds of distributions as well.

Fatima: I know you didn't start like that. You didn't get out of the university and just show up and say, I want to affiliate marketing, I want to do app distribution. Give us a little back-story. How did you get into this field?

Farid: I've been very successful with my own IT business. I used to be a consultant. I left work back in February of 2016. I was very successful in the IT industry. I was a top engineer. I was the go-to guy for design and deployment of infrastructure dealing with huge banks, hedge-funds, pretty much everywhere. Downtown, uptown, midtown Manhattan, New Jersey, Connecticut, so pretty known and well rounded. Dealt with a lot of virtualization, email systems, firewall security, and Storage. Name it I've done pretty much everything you can think of.

Anything that has to do with the data centers, I know how to deal with it. But at some point, I realized I couldn't imagine my family doing the same thing I am doing in case something happens to me. I travel a lot, I take trains every day to go to the city, I'm always in the trenches doing stuff with clients and servers and there's a lot of equipment involved, electricity and heavy machinery and so I said, "what if something happens to me one day and I never come home? What is my family going to do? What is my wife going to do? What are my kids going to do?"

My solution was to build a passive income on the side.

I tried to find something that I can do part-time or on the side like weekends or at night and things like that. I tried a whole bunch of things and I don't know where or how it happened but I landed on affiliate marketing.

In December 2014, I started doing affiliate marketing. From December 2014 until August or September 2015 I had only losses. I kept on losing money, losing money, losing money. There were so many times I was like this is not working. I am just wasting my money. It's not going to happen, it's not going to happen. I kept getting negative, negative, negative comments. My wife was getting upset. She was like okay you are wasting all of our money, what's going on? This is not working so just let it go.

I said no! It has to work. I see everybody else is making it work. I just haven't found the right formula. What happened next, is I met a person who decided to give me some coaching. Since my background is IT, I know IT well and understand technology. I didn't understand marketing as much yet so what I learned was app installs. App installs is very technology-heavy and very little marketing in the mix. That was pretty much right up my alley, and I was able to scale up very rapidly to multiple thousands of dollars in revenue a day.

Going from losing all the time to all of a sudden scaling it up so quickly was the turnaround for me.

That's when I realized -- this is where I need to be. I left my job and started to focus full-time on this.

That's pretty much in a nutshell how I started.

Fatima: What is the most common obstacle preventing people from achieving the outcome that you're experiencing right now in your life?

Farid: I always try to help as many brothers and sisters as I can. I am always giving because I feel like the more you give naturally, things return to you 10 folds. My advice for anybody reading this out there is to stay in your element. Whatever you're good at now, make that work. Once you get that mastered, then you can dabble into other ventures.

Everybody has a skill. You can be a painter, you could be a doctor or engineer, and it could be anybody. Whatever you're good at focus on that and turn that into a passion and a business.

I'll say I'm having so much fun. You need to have the kind of passion for whatever you are doing.

If you are in a job or a work situation where every morning you wake up and you are dreading to go there and you can't wait to go home. You are in the wrong field. You need to figure out what you like to do, what you want to do, where your passion is. The kind of drive that when you wake up and you can't wait to go to work. If you have that and take that information and that knowledge with you and turn it into a business of your own, there's no better combination than that.

Fatima: What would you say to those people who are stuck in jobs; people who always can't wait the day to end, the week to end and only need to get their paychecks because fear is running their lives?

Farid: That's another question that I get a lot from friends and family members. You have to re-evaluate your life. You have to re-evaluate your living standard. The house you live in, the car you're driving, the clothes you're wearing, the food you're eating, the people you're hanging out with. If you are living above your means, you're becoming a slave to your job because the job is what's giving you that security, and that comfort level. You have this false sense of security that you can spend this money today because you're getting that paycheck next week.

If you control yourself, lower your standard of living, live in a smaller house, and get an older car, no need to be eating out every night, or live in your element and your state. Nobody needs to live like a high roller every day. That's just a figment of our imagination. That's just marketing around us. Everybody is telling us to spend more, spend more, and spend more. But what you need to do is save more, save more, and save more. To me, a dollar saved is a dollar earned. The more you can save the more money you can consider that you earned.

Saving is when you can start making some moves and start building a business and invest in your future.

If you are living paycheck to paycheck, you don't have enough money to invest in something. I can't give you any advice because your financial knowledge or financial setup is not correct.

The idea is to live within your means. Save as much as you can in whatever business you're doing. Save whatever money you can and use that money to build a business on the side. If you don't have any money right now and you don't have a job right now I would suggest that you get a skill, whatever that might be. It could be developing websites or taking people's garbage out or driving a car. Drive Uber a couple of days a week or whatever it is. Anything you can do to make some money. You need to make some money, save it, and then start investing it. That's the way you would do business. You can't just say okay I am going to start a business online, set a budget, and then expect it to make a million dollars a week or a month. That's not realistic. Everything has to be calculated. Everything has to be thought out properly, planned, and executed. It doesn't just happen overnight. It takes a lot of work, a lot of focus.

At the same time, if you're not saving money, if you're spending it all on your work and you have expenses so high that you pretty much lock into your paycheck then I would say that you would need to re-evaluate your financial situation.

Fatima: Let's talk a little bit about the family that you came from. You weren't born in a family that had all this consciousness and amazing millionaire mindset. What did you do to get you from a "job mentality" to where you are right now?

Farid: There's a little bit of history behind there. Truth be told I came into this country, in the US in 1992. I came with my mom and my little brother. My little brother was 4 years old back then. My dad came 3 months before us. I was 15 years old by then. I had $10 in my pocket and I said okay I have this money in case my dad is not at the airport I can ask somebody to make a phone call with that money. The job that I was doing wasn't a job. It was a life or death situation.

My dad had no job. We stayed at a place where we had to pay rent. We had no beds or furniture. I was wearing hand me down clothes from other Muslim families in the area. When I went to school, a guy would go "hey that's my shirt you're wearing" and I would go "oh yeah thanks for the shirt". Everything would be all loose on me because I was skinny and small.

Times were rough.

To be able to make it, I had to hustle and the only way I knew to make money was to work. Everything I made paid all the bills, food, rent, all that stuff and I even saved up enough money to buy us a 21-inch T.V. My brother was young and wanted sneakers and Nintendo. I would save up the money to buy him those things because I felt like I had to look after him. Like I said, to me the job was not a job. It was more like a hustle live or die.

I have to work to make that money. Even though I didn't come from a mindset where people talked about business or your own business. My mindset was, work hard. You can say I am a hard worker. I can't sit down and just do nothing. I always have to do something. It all comes down to hard work. A job, it could be a business, your family, put hard work into it. I'm not talking about an hour or two here or there. I mean 18 hours, 17 hours a day you are spending on something. You become an expert. It sounds like I am repeating myself but people see that. People appreciate you; see the value in you, that's how I went from making $3.25 an hour to $180,000 a year. It's because I didn't ask for anything and I worked hard.

People come to me and say hey you are making good progress, you're doing a good job, I'll give you a pay bump, I'm going to make you a manager here, I am going to make you this guy and that guy out of nowhere. I wasn't doing it for that. I was doing it because I liked doing it and I had the hard work ethics that pays off. Then I said okay I have the ethics of working hard, I just need to start working the business model. I got myself a mentor to help me with the business side of things. I said I want the full year of mentorship. Just meeting with him and all the other entrepreneurs in the same room, changed my mindset so much. My hard work combined with this mindset change of working for yourself and building something for you helped me a lot.

Fatima: I want to talk about the failures and the things that you've learned. What did failure teach you and how did it help you grow to who you are today?

Farid: Failure to me is the best teacher. I failed miserably in affiliate marketing, lost a lot of money, got frustrated so many times. But I never gave up. I went out and got myself a teacher, learned a new skill and applied that new skill right away. Everything I have learned in life is due to failing at everything. The more I fail the more I learned about a certain topic and the better I got at it. Any lesson I have learned from my failures I never forget. This is why it's true that failure is the best teacher.

Fatima: Let's talk about your habits. Some habits and rituals can ruin you and hurt you and then rituals and habits that can propel you into success. Share a little bit with us about some of the habits and rituals that you've cultivated on your day-to-day routine and who you are and how you show up as a family man while you build your business

Farid: I think I created workaholic habits. Meaning that I just can't be separated from my computer and business and whatever I am doing. I do spend time with kids and the family of course. What helped me the most is prioritizing what makes or gives me the best ROI on whatever I'm doing. If I were going to do something that takes me three months to get the return I would put that on the back burner. If I can work on something that can give me a result today or tomorrow, I focus on that. I know whatever I'm doing right now I get the result right away as far as the business. Family takes precedence over everything else

Fatima: If somebody was considering going into the app business, what's the first thing a person should do?

Farid: I have two things that I do which are dealing with developers that are like a business and then doing the affiliate marketing. Now the affiliate marketing is something that anybody can get into. I would say that if you have anything less than $10,000 to invest, don't even bother. You need to spend money to gather data, to look at the traffic sources, what traffic works for you, what operating system works, what country works, what browser works, what app or campaign you use or test, what banners to use. There are so many different variables that you need to test and if you are thinking you're going to make money out of the door, it doesn't work that way. It's almost like baking a cake or something and you just going to bake one batch and let people taste it.

They'll say "oh it doesn't taste good!" so you try another one. You've bought the sugar, the flour, you've got the oil, the eggs, and you've baked it. You've got the oven in use, the electricity. You've wasted all these resources and people didn't like it. Now you're going to go buy more ingredients and bake again. You change the formula a little bit and see what happens.

You have to keep trying and trying. Maybe on the 10th try, you'll get one person to say, "Oh it's good." Now you've found that one person that likes your cake. Now what you have to do is find other people that will also like the cake.

You have to spend money initially to find what works before you start making money. So if you have less than $10,000 to invest in the business and there's a lot of moving parts to it, I probably wouldn't bother or try because you're not going to make it. If you're spending $50 a day, you're not going to get the same data as the competition. You're going to get the bottom of the barrel traffic that nobody wants and then you're going to wonder why it's not converting and why people are not installing your apps because you're left with the worst-case scenario. You need to have some budget. Anything below $10K will not work.

Fatima: If people want to get in touch with you and they want to get more information, what is the best way for us to get in touch with you?

Farid: The best way would be to reach out to me on Facebook; my email address is farid@infinitly.com. I also have Snapchat. You can also reach out to me on my websites; apptwo.com or infinitly.com. That's probably the best way to reach me and then follow me around on social media. I'm usually on Facebook. I am very passive. I don't advertise or be in the front but I am reachable if you're out there and you want to connect. And also if I am in your area in any Masterminds or summits, come out and visit, meet up, say hello. I love helping people. I love helping other people to succeed.

ABOUT THE AUTHOR

I work closely with my clients and partners to connect advertisers and mobile application developers to their target audiences. Working with me is different than working with the average mobile marketing team because I can guarantee higher rankings and ratings.

LinkedIn
LinkedIn.com/in/TheFaridKhan

Notes: ✍

Notes:

FARZAN PARUPIA

"To achieve excellence in life, one must achieve balance in a day."

Fatima: Please tell us about your business and the types of customers that you help.

Farzan: Yes I currently have several business ventures. The first is being an online course creator, instructor, and trainer. I've created learning content in a couple of different niches; one is in the Amazon selling niche and the other is in the digital product creating a niche. I first became involved with Amazon as a seller. In mid-2014, I partner with my business mentor to start a private label Amazon business. Fortunately, we were able to grow the business from zero to $50K/month in a matter of only six months. Once people found out about my relatively quick success, they wanted to know how they could start their own Amazon business. So I began helping people for free on a one-on-one basis, answering any questions they had if they contacted me. After a few weeks of doing this, it became infeasible. So a colleague of mine and I decided to conduct a live two-day (weekend) Amazon selling course in Dallas, TX called Marketplace Masters. My partner and I charged $1000 per ticket and about 15 people registered for the course.

It was a great success and this brought even more attention to the business model and increased my credibility as an expert in the Amazon selling space. I received numerous messages and emails from people requesting to somehow receive access to the training materials and resources because they were unable to attend the live course in Dallas. To cater to this great demand, in October of 2015 I decided to create an online course on how to build an Amazon FBA private label business known as EcomEntrepreneurs Academy. The course has done very well with over 200 students worldwide, many of whom have built an Amazon business and achieved excellent results.

After launching my Amazon course on a couple of different occasions, many of my contacts and followers wanted something different. They wanted to launch their own online business, but they didn't want a business model that required a less initial investment. It generally takes about $2-3K to start a private label business on Amazon, and many people wanted something they could start for a few hundred dollars. That's when I put together another online course named Business Launch Academy, which teaches how to create and launch different kinds of digital products, including online courses, apps, software, and eBooks.

Another business venture of mine which I started in mid-2016 is known as Muslim Expert, an online membership platform for Muslim entrepreneurs that contains business and personal development video content and resources. There's an interesting story behind the creation of this platform. When I first became an entrepreneur several years ago, my life started falling apart because I was so busy with my business. I left my full-time job thinking that I would have freedom with my time and money and life would be good. However, I realized the hard way that it takes a lot of time and effort to get to that point. I had to put even more work into my business than I was putting in my full-time job because I had to build it and get it off the ground. For that reason, other areas of my life started suffering, including my family life, my physical health, and my spiritual health. Moreover, my stress levels were at an all-time high and even my involvement in the community was suffering. It was extremely challenging to achieve balance in my life. Balance, in my opinion, means excelling in every area of life, not just one.

At this point, I began talking to other entrepreneurs (including partners and mentors) about my challenges. Little did I know that every one of them faced the same challenges in their way. Some were struggling financially and others spiritually, socially or physically. In nearly every case, it was two or more areas of one's life. I received some advice from those to whom I reached out, but it wasn't enough. I then began reading and researching on the best strategies on how to balance one's life. After a lot of time, effort and struggle and with the blessing and mercy of God, I was able to implement certain daily habits and start balancing my life by excelling in every area of it. I realized that to achieve excellence in life, one must achieve balance in a day.

Once I was able to improve the quality of my own life, I wanted to help my fellow entrepreneurs do the same, knowing that nearly every one of them struggles to achieve the goal of balance and in turn excellence in life. To do this, I decided to create an online video content based membership platform known as Muslim Expert, the goal of which is to merge the gap between business development and personal development for Muslim entrepreneurs.

I am also a business consultant. I began consulting small and medium-sized businesses a few years ago. Interestingly, my biggest client was my first client, Bayyinah Institute, an Arabic education Institution located in Euless, TX. The company's CEO, Norman Ali Khan, is very well known in the Muslim space around the world. Bayyinah conducted live seminars and courses for the first few years of its existence. Then they decided to launch an online platform in mid-2012 known as Bayyinah TV. I began consulting Bayyinah shortly thereafter in marketing Bayyinah TV. In early-mid 2013 I became the Operations Manager of Bayyinah TV and helped the platform grow from six to eight figures per year in revenue in only 24 months.

During my time at Bayyinah, I also became a certified consultant for Infusion soft, a customer relationship management (CRM) software. This software was responsible for much of the company's growth during these two years as I set up many automated and streamlined marketing processes that enabled us to create not one, but two, multi-million dollar marketing campaigns.

My success at Bayyinah and my status as a certified Infusion soft consultant opened the door for me to attract various consulting clients. I have provided many different types of consulting services to small and medium-sized businesses, including book launches, online course and program launches, membership platform launches, online school launches, personal brand growth and much more.

Finally, one aspect of my career that is not as commonly known is my youth work. In 2011, I first began serving the youth by cofounding the youth group at my local Mosque. I was (and still am) very passionate about youth work and voluntarily, I served as the President of the youth group for nearly two years. During this time, I was putting in tens of hours a week and we were able to organize various programs and activities for the youth. We engaged the youth in our community tremendously and we developed many youth activists and leaders. Unfortunately, because there was no paid youth leader opportunity at the time, I had to pursue an opportunity in my field of study (marketing) after I graduated from university.

In October of 2016, a paid opportunity finally came up at my local mosque. They created a full-time paid position for a youth director. Although my goal was never to go back into the "workforce", I didn't consider this as a typical job by any means. Being a youth director is almost like being an entrepreneur except that you're working for an organization. I applied for the position and I got it. Hence, my primary focus currently is engaging and developing the youth and growing the youth group in this local community while my businesses are still running on the side.

Fatima: Give us a little bit of a back story. What you made you go from being a kid, going to university in school, and then coming out and being where you are?

Farzan: Many things have happened that have led me to this point in my career and life. I've always had an interest in the business. I don't know if that's because I am of Pakistani descent, which if you're not aware is an ethnic group that is generally considered cliché for doing business. We are known to own gas stations, convenience stores, and many of us go into business. I don't know if it's that gene, but my dad is a doctor and there are not many business people in my immediate or extended family. Still, for some reason, I had an interest in business as I was growing up and I decided to study business formally in university. What's interesting is that I shifted my focus in business quite a bit. When I started university I was majoring in accounting. Then I switched to management and I eventually settled on marketing as my major (specialization or focus of study).

While I was studying business at Southern Methodist University (SMU) Cox School of Business in Dallas, I was required to do a marketing internship during my final year. I was fortunate enough to do an internship at the Bayyinah Institute in the fall semester of 2012. This was not my initial plan but one day I was at Bayyinah attending an Arabic class, and I started speaking to one of the cofounders of Bayyinah TV, which had launched only about 2 months prior. He told me that they were looking for someone to help them with marketing part-time he interviewed me on the spot. The informal interview went very well and I received an offer letter via email the next day.

I worked as an intern for one semester and then I transitioned into an official part-time job the next semester, which was my final semester of university. Once I graduated from university in May of 2013, I was offered a full-time position at Bayyinah as the Operations Manager of Bayyinah TV. I worked for them for another 2+ years and as I mentioned previously we had a lot of success. Unfortunately as with many growing organizations, politics and many internal issues arose that forced me to search for another opportunity. That's how I got into selling on Amazon.

As with much of my life, I never expected that I would own an Amazon business. In fact, in early 2014 when I was looking for an opportunity to make a side income, I had very little investment capital so my options were limited. But my business mentor who was also my supervisor at Bayyinah had told me about a new business opportunity he was pursuing in October of 2013. He told me that he was taking a $4,000 eight-week course on how to do a specific type of business. He didn't give me any details, but he told me that he'll let me know how it goes. He had experienced some success and he told me that the business model was selling private label products on Amazon. Honestly, I had no idea what he was talking about and I wasn't very interested initially.

But in April of 2014 when the same course opened again for enrollment, my mentor told me that I should sign up. I told him that I don't have $4,000 to invest in the course plus another couple of thousand dollars for the business. He then made me an offer that I could not refuse. He said that he'll partner up with me to start an Amazon business; he'll put up as much investment needed to get the business off the ground. In return, I will do most of the work and manage the business and we'll split it 50/50.

It was an honor and a blessing to be presented with such a proposition. I accepted and it went very well. Within only six months, we were able to reach the six-figure per year in revenue mark. That's when I decided to leave my full-time position and focus entirely on the Amazon business. You know what happened next, as I explained in detail above my various business ventures.

Fatima: Farzan what the main problem faced by people today?

Farzan: There are a few different types of people that approach me when it comes to advising and guidance with business or marketing. The first is someone who has very little to no experience in business but they want to get involved in business and entrepreneurship because they realize we are currently in the midst of a revolution; so much money is being made online and it can be done so with minimal risk, fairly little time involvement and very low upfront cost. So many people ask me about the types of business opportunities that are available that they can utilize to make a good side income. This side income could potentially in the future (in a few months or years) replace one's full-time income, making it much easier to have flexibility with one's time, money and life. Hundreds of thousands, if not millions, of people around the world, have achieved this goal of becoming full-time self-dependent entrepreneurs. That's the first type of person.

The second type is someone who has a business idea or has an existing business or perhaps has some experience in business but they failed, or they haven't reached the level at which they aspire to be. Hence they contact me for tips on marketing and on other areas of business that will help them succeed or succeed at a higher level.

Marketing is such an essential part of any business; it is the tool using which one attains leads and customers, which of course is the means to make a profit. Unfortunately, most amateurs or even most business owners, in general, do not see the value and the power of marketing, and they don't realize that it's the tool that will get you clients and leads and customers, which is what you need to make money as a business. I know many people on a personal level, locally and internationally, who have gone into business and they don't have a budget for marketing. For some reason, they think that "word of mouth" is going to suffice when it comes to growing and building a business and that's simply not the case. You have to invest in your business, you have to pay for advertising, promotions, and marketing to be able to grow a business. I think one of the primary causes of business failure, whether online or offline is the lack of marketing altogether or lack of placing enough importance on marketing.

The third type of person is someone who is much more experienced in business than in the first two types. The other two types are less experienced or have no experience while this third type is more experienced, but they need help taking their business to the next level. If one's business already makes six figures a year, the owner wants to take it to the next level: seven figures. This can be done by improving or scaling marketing efforts, do a new massive product launch or any number of things.

Fatima: What is the most common obstacle preventing them from increasing their sales, moving up to the next notch, and getting their message out there?

Farzan: The most common obstacle preventing entrepreneurs from increasing their sales is mindset; simply not believing that they can get to the next level, thinking that what they've achieved is their full potential. However, one can always push above and beyond it and reach a higher potential.

The second most common obstacle is perfectionism. The majority of entrepreneurs are aiming for perfection. I believe you should aim for excellence, not perfection. Because of this tendency, an entrepreneur ends up working on a program or a course for two years without still having launched it. Aiming for perfection costs an entrepreneur a lot of time, money and effort. The advice I give everyone is at least put something out and then you can improve it and "perfect" it later. One of the business mentors always tells me, "Imperfect action is better than perfect inaction." The most important thing is getting your offering out there. As the saying goes, money loves speed.

A quick story that Grant Cardone shared at a conference I attended at which he was a speaker… He said that when he was writing his first book, he was working on it for months. He eventually got fed up with himself and the delay in publishing and launching his book that he committed that he will write the entire book in one afternoon, and whatever he has done at the end of that afternoon, he will submit it to the editor and publish the book. His first book incidentally went on to become a best seller. That's not the best part. Shortly after he launched his book and it became a best-seller, he was approached by someone who started telling him about the hundreds of spelling, punctuation and formatting mistakes that he found in Grant's book. He spent hours doing this and even made a list of all the errors. Grant responded by saying, "This is the bestselling book, not a best-written book!" Of course, he fixed all the mistakes that were found in the book, but he did it later after he first launched it. I remember this story whenever I tend to exhibit perfectionist tendencies and it helps me keep in mind that it's more important to take action as quickly as possible even if it's imperfect.

The third most common obstacle as I mentioned previously is marketing, or the lack thereof. This refers to not enough effective marketing or perhaps a lack of importance placed on marketing. I believe this root from people relying too heavily on their existing level knowledge and/or experience; they've done things previously in a certain way and because it worked well they want to continue doing it the same way, with very little innovation. If you're not innovating when it comes to your offerings, product launches and in conducting business in general, it will difficult to get to another level. That's because for your business to get to another level, you're thinking, your strategy, and your marketing must also get to another level to be able to achieve the higher-level results that you desire. Much of marketing is tactical and strategic (the launches, the funnels, the email automation, etc.) and must be learned by an entrepreneur to succeed in business.

The fourth most common obstacle is fear, which is similar to the mindset. There are many different types of fear. One fear is about what other people are going to say, and the thought (or doubt) that the idea will not be receptive or liked by most people. Another type of fear risk, whether it's with an investment of one's time, money or effort. There's no guarantee that one will succeed so the fear of failure prevents many people from starting in the first place. Yet another type of fear is fear of growth and change. If someone is already a successful business owner, to take it to the next level one may have to make a large financial investment into marketing or hiring to achieve one's future goals. It's easy to become comfortable which lowers one's tendency to take the risk. But it's important to realize that this fear, and all fears for that matter, lives within our minds. We are only limited by that which we limit ourselves.

Fatima: Did you grow up in a family who were big thinkers? Or was there a process for you to go through that expanded your mind and beliefs to where you are now today?

Farzan: There wasn't too much of a business presence or practice of entrepreneurship in my direct or extended family. I didn't have that, to begin with. It was an interest that I had on my own and it grew as I grew older. Then I decided to study business formally in university and there has been a process of growth from having to learn everything on my own. On a general level though, although there weren't many entrepreneurs in my family, my dad being a doctor has worked very hard his entire life. Every medical professional has gone through such a rigorous journey to get to where they are. And my mother played a pivotal role in my outlook on life and business as well. Being a stay at home mom of multiple children and a homemaker, she has worked harder than anyone I know. That kind of work ethic, dedication, commitment and desire for success from my parents translated to me, and these principles apply to any field.

Furthermore, my parents struggled a lot migrating to this country and then having to make a place and a name for themselves in the local community. That helped my initial background tremendously when I was growing up. As a result of my parents' efforts to provide the best of everything for their children, I was blessed to live in a great neighborhood surrounded by great company (friends and community leaders).

Then when I began working in the business and marketing field professionally, there was another process of growth, primarily self-learning. I had to learn to expand my mindset. When I first started a business, my goal was to build a five-figure business. But as I learned more, networked with more people and found mentors, I realized I was thinking way too small. I then began thinking about building a six, seven or even eight-figure business. Another aspect of this growth was networking and connecting with others. I used to think that I could do everything on my own. I would think, "It's my business and if I do the work and focus on putting in effort and time I'll be good." I didn't put enough importance on networking and connecting with other people who I could potentially collaborate or partner within business, or simply connecting with them and having them available to help or support me whenever needed, or vice versa of course. I've learned over time how to develop these crucial connections. And I've seen the massive impact having great connections can have not only when it comes to business, but in any area of life.

Another huge learning process for me has been my relationship with money. There have been times since I became an entrepreneur several years ago when I made a good amount of money with a product or course launch, or as an affiliate for someone else's offering. Then for some reason due to my lack of maturity and understanding at that time about how money works and the language of money, I would eventually start running short on funds. Then I would focus and make a good amount of money again but it would come back down again in a few months. This up and down spectacle was a huge struggle and I've had to learn to handle money more carefully and invest it instead of spending it to ensure that my business income is consistent. I think a lot of entrepreneurs face this challenge like me because they get excited when they make some money on their own as an entrepreneur and they don't know how to handle it properly.

Another aspect of the journey has to do with business goals and passion. A lot of entrepreneurs struggle with this and are always thinking about how to align their business goals with their passion. This is because when it comes to business, there's an aspect of making money and another aspect of enjoying what you do and contributing not only with the money that you make in the business but with the business itself as a contribution to society and the world. I think often people are stuck in a position in which they want to do something that makes money and also caters to their desire and passion. That's also something with which I've been struggling. The Muslim Expert platform, for example, is the closest I have gotten to something that makes money (business goal) and also helps people because (my passion) as it's based on my struggle in balancing my business/work and personal life.

ABOUT THE AUTHOR

Farzan Parupia is an entrepreneur who helps fellow entrepreneurs achieves their full potential in their businesses and their lives. He serves others with his business and marketing expertise, talents and knowledge. Simply put, Farzan loves helping others succeed. Farzan has utilized his skills to build million-dollar marketing funnels and campaigns for companies such as  Bayyinah Institute. He is currently involved in several business ventures.

First, Farzan is an e-commerce business owner - he sells physical products online, primarily on Amazon. He was able to grow his business from zero to six-figures/year in revenue in a matter of only six months.

Second, Farzan is an online course creator. After building his own successful Amazon business, Farzan committed himself to help others do the same with his online course, EcomEntrepreneurs Academy. Hundreds of students have taken this course and achieved results within months. Farzan has also created an online course named Business Launch Academy to help entrepreneurs launch a digital business.

Third, Farzan is a business consultant, certified by Digital Marketer in several specializations. Previously an Infusion soft Certified Partner, he helps small and medium-sized businesses take their revenue generation and marketing processes to the next level. His most notable achievement is helping Bayyinah TV, an online Arabic education platform, grow from six to eight figures/year in revenue in only two years. His primary expertise and passion are in building profitable marketing funnels, marketing automation, and email marketing.

Fourth, Farzan is the founder and CEO of Muslim Expert, a business and personal development platform whose goal is to help 10,000 Muslim entrepreneurs build a profitable business and lead a balanced life in 10 years.

Fifth and finally, Farzan is a public speaker. He has spoken on many stages and platforms to thousands of audience members. He frequently delivers talks, lectures, speeches, and sermons (which can be found on YouTube) in many different types of gatherings.

Notes:

HADAYAI MAJEED

"Do not be afraid to live. Trust in God and what He has given you"

Hadayai Majeed is the director of the Baitul Salaam Network. Hadayai helps and assists families in the Muslim community on the issue of abuse. She understands the plight and the problems of Muslim clients and she helps Muslim women to regain their pride and dignity so they can reinvent their lives after divorcee, abuse, and violence. All proceeds of this book will be donated to BaitulSalaam.org

Fatima: It's a pleasure to have you here. Can you tell us a little bit about the charity and the types of people that you help?

Hadayai: Baitul Salaam is an international Domestic Violence Awareness organization. We assist with educating primarily the Islamic community about the issue of domestic abuse. We work with local social workers and organizations outside the Islamic community to help them understand better the needs of their Muslim clients. We also provide direct services. We distribute food twice a week. And once a year, around Christmas time, we host a toy drive and those toys go to children from low-income households, and we also work with the low income elderly, and pretty much that's what we do.

F: How did you get into this field? Was there some kind of journey that inspired you to be this kind of a woman; directing and facilitating this kind of aide?

Hi: My mother was a social worker and she was involved in projects such as relocating people from Vietnam when they came over in the early '70s in various types of community and neighbourhoods. The journey that brought me to where I am now is I am also a survivor of domestic abuse, and as a Muslim and I know how difficult it was for me to get the assistance I needed when I was in crisis. There was so much misunderstanding about the issue and survivors of domestic abuse.

F: When a woman is having this kind of problem or crisis, what do you think is the most common obstacle that is preventing her from getting the support she needs at the time?

H: It's knowing where to go and having someone like a case manager that can be compassionate and be there with them. Just general ignorance as far as a lot of people in leadership in our community. A lot of people think they know what domestic violence is and they don't. Some women are told just be more patient, go home and take a nice bath, put on something pretty or nice cologne and things will change.

F: What do you think is the biggest misconception of people outside the community looking at abused women?

H: From the outside of our community, it's just a misunderstanding about Islam in general. They think that Islam teaches that women are less than second-class citizens and that it is taught. A lot of them feel like since it's taught and you are part of that religion, you are in someplace where you are not valued.

F: So you have the Muslim community who doesn't understand what this woman is going through and then you have the larger community who says you're a Muslim and that's what your religion teaches you. Is that accurate?

H: Pretty much. Now that we have had the terror attacks and 9-11, a lot of political news and misunderstanding about Islam in general, a lot of people think that Islam is just the in Middle East like Saudi Arabia. They don't realize that a person can be Muslim and come to you from any part of the world, including the large population we have now in the United States, which I would say are about 50% converted to Islam. They just fear them. When people fear things they do things they wouldn't normally say or do.

F: What kind of role do you play when it comes to helping women overcome some of the misconceptions and get back on their feet so she can feel safe for herself and her kids?

H: Our organization just began working with people where they are. There's no judgment. We are there to be good sisters, to give them valid information and to hold their hands until they can navigate and negotiate their way through what they need to go through. For example, when women need to go to court to get protection orders, we help train her in Metro Atlanta with one of the best-funded domestic violence organizations in the state and that particular organization has advocated in court twice a week so we walk through what they will have to do, the types of questions they'll have to answer, what will be expected of them. They will need to be in court, in front of the judge and restate what has happened. Then the forms are filled out and they'll go over to the sheriff's department and the sheriff's department will ask a few questions and then they will send the order out. The judge will approve the order and then the order is hand-delivered to the abuser. We also explain to them what that order means.

It is a legal document and everything in it has to be followed. If not, it will become null and void. Many people who come to us are not ready to do that, they go through the initial step and then it's three or four days later, it's a week or 2 weeks later. Some perpetrator calls them and says they are sorry, they will offer a gift, and say it won't happen again. Then some other family members will talk to them and say, "You know that's not the right thing to do, you don't want to turn a Muslim man over to the authority here because of the misunderstandings that many of them have towards us here in this country. It's going to be okay and we will help you. Drop it." Often, many of them will drop it because they feel the family members are going to come in, the local community is going to come in, and everything is going to be all right. Unfortunately, what happens is everything is all right for maybe a couple of months then they trigger a negative reaction and the abuser starts all over again. Some Muslim women feel they are being punished for something they did wrong when their marriage isn't going the way that it is supposed to be. They are being punished for going to the authority because they are encouraged to protect the perpetrator.

F: Tell me a little bit about yourself. What did you do to leave an abusive situation, turn your life around and put yourself in a position where you are now helping women to be free and safe?

H: I think it was a little easier for me because I born and raised here in the United States. I came from a family where abuse doesn't happen. I just had to get over the initial guilt of blaming myself for the relationship going bad. What was it I didn't hear or see? Once I got over that, which didn't take long, I was able to start my steps moving forward. What was confusing for me as a Muslim was, I had been a Muslim two years when my crisis started and it took me to realize that people are humans. It doesn't matter how they dress, how they pray, where they pray at, they're humans. Once I separated Muslims as human beings from Muslims that are angels I was able to move forward into what I felt was needed for myself. I am not exactly sure what happened to make me get this brilliant idea that we needed service in our community and that I would be the one being a part of getting it started. I'm going to be very honest with you, I thought after we had our first meeting, it was four of us, and we all four had been in some type of crisis. One of us is a recovering alcoholic, the other was a mom in an abusive situation, mostly verbal abuse and she's selfish. She says she would make it work until her children got older so they wouldn't be part of a split family and then there was another young mom, who had pretty much been abandoned. She was struggling day by day trying to raise two of her sons on her own and not having any help or child support because her husband was from another country. All of the legal services here could not help her be able to get child support from him. Exactly what made me think that should I be the one doing this?

F: Some of the best things that come out are in the stage of craziness or madness and you just get that jolt of electricity and you don't think about it too much, you just get it done.

H: That's pretty much true. I also found that after we put the notice out the sisters who were social workers and counsellors, attorneys and judges and even some brothers who had those skills can step forward and help. I didn't think that I would here after 19 years and to be the one who they called. We have a lot of master level social workers here; we have a few with PHD's. We have a Ph.D. psychologist, the MD psychiatrist. I just knew someone so skilled and experienced would be the one to step up and be the one leading.

F: Hadayai let's talk about failure, pain, obstacles, and challenges. How has all that failure and pain helped you to grow and be the woman that you are today?

H: I just had to face that pain, the reality, and work through it. Know that it's a part of life, accept my role in it, but at the same time not beat me up. I am not the only woman who ever made a mistake choosing my husband. I am not the only woman who has found herself rejected by a man in some way. I am not the only woman who saw herself homeless in America. About 50% of the women who are homeless in

America, are due to domestic violence and leaving home. It's a reality. Holding onto my faith as well as going to workshops and reading self-help books. Just the journey of holding onto the love of God and getting through it.

F: As you look over your life now, what would you say to your younger self?

H: I would say do not be afraid to live. Hold onto your faith. Do not put people on a pedestal because that's not where they belong. Trust in God and what he's given you. If you feel something is wrong then move away from it. Do not be afraid to open doors and do not be afraid to hold onto the opportunity. Just do not be afraid. Do not live in fear.

F: Successful people talk about habits and rituals that can break you and habits and rituals that can propel you into success. Tell us a little bit about what habits and rituals you created that keep you grounded, calm and focused on the work that you're doing?

H: Praying. Reading the Holy Book and listening to presentations of the Holy Book. Working out and making myself physically fit as I can be. I love to read and listen to new ideas and I just look forward to the next phase of my life. I look forward to being an elderly woman and I'm not afraid of it. I just want to be healthy so that means I have to eat healthily and not storing up on a lot of sweets. I have to love myself. I need to be able to look into the mirror and love everything that I see. My skin color, my features, my hair color. Just love myself and if I see something that needs to be improved then start improving on it.

F: What can you say to those women that are stuck and suffering in violent abusive relationships?

H: Everyone is not going through it, it's not normal, and no you don't have to stay in it. You just have to hold on to your faith, or whatever you call your faith. Know that the creator doesn't want you to be hurt, the creator didn't create you to be something that someone wipes their feet on, the creator loves you and the creator doesn't make mistakes. It's going to be difficult, it won't be easy but you can do it. You can make up your mind that you're no longer going to be abused and that means someone yelling at you all the time, someone calling you ugly names, someone hitting you, sitting on you, or whatever. You do not have to accept that as a way of life. The creator has more for you and whatever your faith is grab onto that faith and move forward.

F: Thank you. Hadayai, if someone wants to work with you or donate money, how can they get in touch?

H: Thank you. We have a website and that's www.BaitulSalaam.org there's a donate button on that site and it goes to our PayPal system. They can use PayPal if they are a member or not so PayPal will take their credit card or banking information.

They can also mail donations to us at Baitul Salaam Network PO Box 115470, Atlanta Georgia 30310.

They can also call us if they have questions at 770-255-8500.

If you want to be a volunteer, you can get in touch with us via Facebook because we do have online volunteers and there are a lot of things that you can do from your home or wherever you happen to be, in any part of the world where there's the internet.

If you are a local in Metro Atlanta just give us a call at 770-255-8500. We have a small office located inside the Fulton County Life Center at 3300 Memorial Drive, Suite 5. Our door is at the back of the building. We're in the office on Tuesdays and Thursdays from 12noon to 2 pm. We can stay later if you need us to stay.

We can also arrange to meet you at other locations if coming into our office is not convenient for you. We meet people at the local Mosques, pharmacy centers, restaurants, cafes, wherever it is comfortable with you for the first meeting. We're flexible.

F: That's great! Thank you so much for all that information. It has been so enlightening to speak with you this afternoon. Hadayai are there any last thoughts you would like to share?

H: My prayer is that when I retire, other people step up. Not necessarily one person but people should step up and get the training because you can do this work wherever you are and all you need to do is call or email haleem1@aol.com and we'll be glad to talk with you about what you need to do to be effective in this work. The main thing wants to do it. The second is listening and learning certain skills that you will need to learn and be resilient. Know that you are doing the right thing.

ABOUT THE AUTHOR

Hadayai Majeed's vision is both simple and huge: give Muslim women the tools to change their climate by changing themselves. A member of a religion that is focused on service, Hadayai was called to reach out to her sisters, and in 1997 she founded Baitul Salaam Network, Inc. to help victims of domestic abuse. The goal of the  network is to end the silence about domestic violence and to help abused Muslim women and children with shelter, food, and clothing. The organization also teaches strategies for self-sufficiency: how to be confident in speech, mannerisms, and body language.

Hadayai Majeed's marriage was one of neglect and denigration. But when she sought intervention, counsel, encouragement, and financial assistance from Muslim families and friends, she was told she was at fault. The policy of the community's one shelter was to tell abused women to be quiet and to "move on". Instead, Hadayai saw a need and she moved to fill it. Although her mother was a social worker, Hadayai had avoided following in her footsteps, observing its demands. But in 1997, she responded to the call of her faith and founded Baitul Salaam. The vision of Baitul Salaam is to provide a community in which women are self-empowered through their spiritual beliefs and which respects the rights and liberties of every person. Baitul Salaam Network operates at local, state, and national levels: requests for help are frequent. Locally, the network focuses on providing shelter as well as training in prevention and intervention. Information about the program is widely disseminated on bulletin boards in mosques, Islamic centers, and on the Internet. Hadayai is a frequent presenter at her mosque in Atlanta and national conferences and women's gatherings. She is a recognized resource concerning abused and neglected Muslim women and children for social workers, mental health professionals, and abuse victims' advocates throughout the state of Georgia. Hadayai has been challenged by a lack of cooperation from some Muslim leaders, who interpret her work as "rebellious". Nevertheless, her group has succeeded in making domestic violence awareness a focus of national conferences, and some local leaders now give khutbahs (Friday prayer lectures) to raise awareness about the issue. The network and its leaders have received formal recognition from several Muslim organizations and the state of Georgia.

Baitul Salaam Network, Inc.

Notes:

KHALIAH HALL TRAWALLY

"Don't fear! A big vision, determination, and your faith in God will pull you forward."

Fatima: Khaliah let's talk about your business. Tell us about the kind of business that you do right now.

Khaliah: Currently, I coach permissible real-estate investment strategies to Muslim women in the US. I teach them everything from A to Z, such as how to find motivated sellers and distressed properties, how to build your motivated seller lists, how to persuade sellers, how to secure the deal, and how to collaborate with other investors. Women learn the steps required to close a deal in 60 days or less

F: What led you to this field?

K: I went to school for industrial engineering. So my first job was an engineer. I hated my job. I spent three hours of commuting every day. I spent most of my time trying to figure out what I was going to do with the rest of my life. I knew what I was doing wasn't what I wanted to do. I would say it was God that led me to real estate. While I was working my 9 to 5, I met a friend. She's a longtime friend and business partner. She quit her 9 to 5 and was studying to get a real estate license. That's what sparked my interest initially and then I also started learning about real estate myself. I was bored on my job and eventually, it got to the point where one day I went to work and I quit. I didn't spend a lot of time delaying and deliberating about it, I went in and quit.

Ironically enough, I was offered another job the same day that I quit. But I turned it down.

From there I started taking some classes. One day, someone in the class told me they knew of someone who coaches how to invest in real estate. I got their phone number. I called them, and they told me what I needed to do to find and close deals. I did exactly what they told me to do step by step and was able to close deals. From then on, I never looked back. I have been in real-estate since 2003. So basically, I would say meeting like-minded people is what sparked my interest and got me into real estate. It wasn't anything I went to school for and I enjoy it. I enjoy the flexibility that it offers. Since I started 2003, I've done real estate coaching, sales, appraisals, land lording, flipping, wholesaling, and taken real estate coursework at John's Hopkins.

F: If there's a woman out there Khaliah who's saying I want to do this and I want to invest in real estate. I've put a little bit of money aside. What do you see in some of the people that you work with as the most common obstacle preventing them from being successful?

K: I would say mindset is the biggest obstacle. I meet people who are always so excited to get into the business but when they find out that being successful in real estate requires hard work they easily get discouraged and quit. If you don't have a lot of time, then you need to have more money to outsource your responsibilities. For example, I've had students who had no experience do a deal in 3 weeks and then quit what they were doing that got them results. I don't know if it's because they feel it can't be repeated or… I would say mindset is the biggest obstacle.

F: And how can they overcome that? How can they get over that to successfully achieve the outcome of working with you?

K: That's a good question. I would say the main thing that they would probably need to do is being open-minded and also being able to take direction. Everyone always has their doubts when starting something new but I think if you keep an open mind and be open to what someone is asking you to do or telling you that you need to do and take a step forward, then it helps you to overcome that. Then you start to see that maybe what you were thinking and what needs to happen are two different things.

F: If they follow your lead and keep an open mind, is this going to work?

K: Right and I think that's why I was able to stay in the business for so long. When I first got started I had a coach as well and I just did what he told me to do. It wasn't extraordinary because of course, you are kind of just repeating a process. Even the strategies and things that I am teaching, it's nothing new. It's being able to apply the things that you're learning. When I got started, for example, my mentor told me what to do and I did what he told me. I got to see that it does work. It's just about following instructions.

F: Not everyone is born into a family with parents that are open-minded and entrepreneurs. Most people grow up in homes where they learn to be safe and have a regular 9-5 job. What did you do to transform your beliefs?

K: I would say probably having faith. It's interesting because I would say that getting into real estate is part of my journey to Islam. I grew up as a Christian and I'm actually the only Muslim in my family and so it's been an interesting journey for me. My mentor's wife is the one who introduced me to Islam. I would pray to God and I knew that this is what I wanted to do and move forward. No matter what other people say. My family is not supportive all the time, but if I knew I was going to do something I would just make sure that I kept doing whatever I was going to do to get to whatever my goal was.

I've had a lot of obstacles with family, especially having a younger child. I remember times when I was meeting with sellers and I would ask someone to babysit and they would say no. Mainly because they didn't support me being an entrepreneur. A couple of times I even had to take my daughter with me on appointments. I had a business partner at the time and so he would come with me. We would take turns playing with her while we were talking with the seller. We started calling my daughter closer. We found that when people saw kids they would let their guard down and so they were easier to deal with as far as selling. I didn't take no for an answer. If someone wasn't willing to do something for me then I would make another way to make it happen.

F: Let's talk about failure, obstacles, challenges, falling. How has failure and pain helped you to grow?

K: It's helped me tremendously. I would say some of my biggest obstacles. One was dealing with employees because at some point I had a full team of 12 people or so before I traveled to West Africa in 2014. It wasn't an easy experience as far as training people and then having people execute whatever you needed to be done for your business. Sometimes I would put a lot of trust in certain people and they would kind of let me down so it helped me to overcome. Also, I would say not being attached to the outcome. Not being attached to the outcome has helped me to move forward. I feel like if someone does something and you're attached to it then it brings you down but if you're not attached to it, and someone does something you can accept it and still move forward.

F: What would you say to your younger self?

K: My younger self? Well, I would say probably have more faith. I would have never expected when I was younger that I would have converted to Islam because I didn't know what Islam was all about. I would say have more faith because I had to deal with a lot of… growing up and stuff I didn't have a lot of confidence. Those are not things that I had. I was always smart with books and things like that and education but I didn't have a lot of confidence and I think that stemmed from my lack of faith.

F: Do you mean like faith in God or faith in your abilities?

K: Well both because I didn't necessarily… I had a connection to God but I didn't know what it meant to have faith so I didn't know… even for instance just having faith to be able to move forward, knowing that you're going to be okay.

I think that's the whole thing with even quitting my job. When I quit my job I didn't even have a plan so I had to have the faith to take the next step that God was going to be able to provide for me. I think that's the connection that I had to make, that if you have faith and you take the next step you're going to be okay because God is going to help you. That's something that I had to learn when I was younger. I didn't understand that connection.

F: What are some of the rituals and habits that you've created in your life outside of your prayer that have solidified your position as a real estate investor and helping other women do the same?

K: I would say the biggest one is just being very committed. For instance, I used to do a lot of seminars in public before I started working with Muslim women. I was pretty much just working with people locally and so all different types of people. Every Saturday I would be very committed to just going out and having these seminars. Of course, they were info seminars so they were free. I wasn't necessarily getting paid for it but I just had to be very consistent. Every week or every two weeks I was always doing seminars. It wasn't easy to want to get out and go do things when you're not being compensated. I would just say being consistent. Let's say I'm calling sellers or someone that wants to sell their house, just being very consistent about my work ethics.

F: What did consistency do for you in your business and positioning?

K: Well it did everything because from that I was able to see the fruits of my labor. Sometimes I wouldn't necessarily see things happening, I wouldn't have always been able to anticipate what was going to happen on the back end, but I was able later to see the fruits of my labor. Each time when I was having a seminar if I was looking for new students to work with or new clients to work with eventually… what happens is since people are coming to these lectures they were able to see that I was an expert in what I was talking about those people would want to work with me. I was able to see the fruits of my labor from that.

F: Khaliah if there's a woman out there that wants to do business with you, what would be the first thing that she needs to be ready for to either work with you or to do this kind of thing?

K: The first thing is I would say having the mindset and just knowing that this is what you want to do. I would say that's the first thing that needs to happen before you even decide to take the steps further.

F: And once she has her mindset ready? What's the next most important thing she needs to be ready for?

K: I would say to be able to work hard and put in some work. On average when you are first getting started, you need to be able to out in at least 10-20 hours a week. I would say the first thing is to be able to work hard and be ready to do some work.

F: How can we find out more about you and what's the best way for us to connect with you?

K: You can call me on at 202-378-0258 or you can also go to my website. It's khaliahhalltrawally.me I can also be found on facebook https://www.facebook.com/KhailahHallTrawally/ and Instagram @khaliahhtrawally

F: Any last-minute thoughts on real-estate investing?

K: I would say don't be afraid. Feel free to contact me if you have any questions. Let's say there are things you never thought of or considered don't be afraid to ask questions. You can ask me anything that you want.

F: Wonderful. Thank you Khaliah. It has been such a pleasure speaking with you.

ABOUT THE AUTHOR

Khaliah Hall Trawally's background consists of studying as an Industrial Engineer at Morgan State University. She received a Bachelor's of Science in 2001. After receiving her degree, she went to work as an Industrial Engineer at Northrop Grumman and later become a Cost Estimator with Naval Sea Systems Command in 2002. She left her career as  an Engineer in 2003 and became a Landlord and Real Estate Wholesaler. She has completed real estate coursework at Johns Hopkins. In addition to having real estate appraisal and commercial inspection experience, she became licensed as a full-time Real Estate Agent in 2005 and opened a real estate brokerage, City Dwellers, focused primarily on real estate investing with her business partner.

Since 2005, Khaliah and her associates have completed over $60 Million in Sales. In 2014, she was recognized in the 3rd Edition of Who's Who in Black Washington, DC and had the opportunity to travel to The Gambia and Senegal to study the culture, real estate market, and development. To-date, Khaliah has over a decade of experience in the commercial and residential real estate industries. Since returning to the United States, Khaliah specializes in coaching Muslim women to invest in real estate.

You can reach her at her website www.queenrealestateinvestors.com

Her email is reiwithKhaliah@gmail.com

Notes:

NABILLAH FAROOQ

"Change your direction overnight and stand out embracing yourself."

Fatima: Nabillah, please tell me about your business and the type of customers that you help.

Nabillah: I am the 'PCOS weight management Coach' and Founder at 'Be Fit-The Prophet's Way'. I help overwhelmed and frustrated women and girls overcome PCOS weight issues through the language of food.

I had PCOS myself when I was 16 yrs old. It started with strange-looking acne and I remember I stopped going out for 2 months! I didn't go to my school as well that's when my parents took me to various health practitioners in hope of curing my acne till I read Islamic medicine, Muslim Guidance and found the cure in it for both acne and PCOS. (Polycystic ovarian disease or syndrome)

Since then I have helped Muslim sisters and I feel honored and content each time we celebrate a milestone successfully achieved by a sister, especially when they share their success story of being a mom to their first healthy child.

F: Tell us a little bit about your journey.

N: I was a victim of this symptom during my teen years. No one in my family had this, it was just me. It started with me at 16 years of age with menstrual irregularities. I skipped my schooling for months because of heavy bleeding and cystic acne. I stopped socializing mostly because of my cystic acne. My acne was not like regular pimples. It was very different. One pimple would grow and then coalesce with neighboring ones to form a large ugly crusty pimple. In 10 days the large pimple would dry out and fall off but with a deep scar on my facial skin. My parents took me to various health practitioners but to no benefit. Then my menstrual irregularities became worse. I was 18 years old by then and to make matters worse I was also a picky eater. I ended up having chronic anemia with Hemoglobin just 4 g/dl and was transfused with 1 pint of blood. I was not pleased with my health and I felt bad for not taking care of my body and health. This is when I started studying researching PCOS on my own. I was formally diagnosed with PCOS by an ultrasound scan at the age of 18. It revealed cysts in the ovaries. My hormonal profile was normal at first then later got disturbed. By this time, I was also preparing to enter medical school, thinking that I would be able to cure my PCOS. Little did I know that modern medicine didn't know the cause of PCOS. So all therapy is focused on treating the symptoms. Applying band-aid to the wound was not a satisfactory option for me. This increased my interest to find the root cause of PCOS even more because a Muslim Guidance kept popping up in my mind and made me kind of more curious.

The Holy Quran says:

> "There is no disease that God has created, except that He also has created its remedy." ~Bukhari 7.582

Long story short, I spoke to various health professionals including my professors at teaching hospital, homeopaths, clinical dieticians, endocrinologists, read many studies done on PCOS, been part of various PCOS community groups etc. Until I started studying Islamic medicine, The Prophet's nutrition and combined all my allopathic and Islamic medical knowledge and through my trial and errors found the way to overcome PCOS and the vicious cycle that comes with it for life. I was 23 years old by then and by age of 26 yrs got married. As most women with PCOS are fertility challenged, so I and my husband decided to complete our family by having children. I kept my focus on having faith in God and doing what I had to do to conceive while keeping my PCOS at bay. Within 7 years of marriage, we had our 4 energetic children while I was studying further and working as well.

1 in 5 woman suffer with this syndrome. It's actually metabolic syndrome that upsets the endocrine system (hormonal system). So the problem begins within our stomachs that leads to symptoms like weight gain, irregular periods, acne, hair thinning and hair fall, male pattern hair growth, stress, depression, suicidal, hypothyroid, pilonidal sinus, psoriasis, diabetes, fertility challenge whether it's difficulty conceiving or sustaining, etc. I know modern medicine uses the term infertility but sisters with PCOS are not infertile, they are just fertility challenged.

I have read various books on our beloved Prophet's life and the way our Prophet and the wife of Prophet did business, and how they served people through their business.

I try my best to follow in their footsteps and I am content where I stand today.

I had spent just $5000 to start my business including the required business training. Most importantly, I love doing my business from my home office while I get to enjoy each moment with our children as they grow and learn with us.

F: What have you found has been the biggest misconception and pitfall for these women that have been struggling for so many years?

N: Most of the time it's the wrong food choices, without knowing what type of PCOS they have. Another misconception is that medicines (oral contraception pills, Glucophage, etc.) will cure PCOS for life.

Medicines only help with symptoms and once they come of the medicine, they relapse.

If they manage to get pregnant, it will cure their PCOS. Permanent cure only happens when the root cause is treated.

Most of the sisters think that what worked for one sister will work for her as well. The fact is, it will work only if it is aimed at treating the cause of PCOS or else it's like applying a band-aid on the wound without treating the wound.

Upon joining my program sisters do share their frustration of feeling stuck and depressed as medicines don't work and weight doesn't come of although they have been at the gym for the whole year. They have been through all sorts of treatment options available including the invasive procedures, like drilling their ovaries. Some have feared that if they don't conceive, their husbands will abandon them. They are very fragile emotionally as PCOS does make them fertility challenged.

Having the right mindset is very important for achieving any kind of success in our lives whether it's our health or our businesses.

My advice for sisters is - find out what is the cause of their PCOS. We can't solve the problem if we are not aware of what's causing it.

Find out why they have PCOS instead of relying on an internet search.

1. To get educated about the PCOS and its types.

2. Understand how medicines work and why medicines are not the solution and why sisters are not able to conceive with medicines that are prescribed for their PCOS.

F: Nabillah tells us about the process when a client first comes to you.

N: On joining the program, the first step is to fill out assessment forms. This allows me to look into each body system and find out which body system is not in harmony with the rest of the systems.

The second step is to create an action plan to help them overcome weight issues & PCOS via food, workouts, tools & tips, medicinal bleeding, lifestyle medication (if required) and education (via online classes).

As PCOS doesn't happen overnight therefore, it takes some time to heal as well. So it takes anywhere from one to twelve months to overcome PCOS and get at, healthy and energetic.

F: Did you grow up in a family where everybody was an entrepreneur and researching new things and curious about life? Tell us a little about your mind and your beliefs and how you got to be the woman that you are today.

N: Yes I grew up in a home where all my family members are into business. My grandparents had their own business. My husband runs his Real Estate business and IT Banking System Consultancy Business. My father and my two brothers are Electric Engineers and have their Engineering Consultancy Businesses. My younger sister runs her own online IT Consultancy Business while enjoying being the mom to 7 years old son. My father always stressed that for successful business having university education is important along with knowledge of Deen. Without knowledge of Deen, personal development is incomplete. I think having a business that helps others out is the best. I had been unconsciously doing this throughout my life, even the time while I was growing up at my parent's home. I have been helping friends, relatives' neighbors, using my knowledge and skills. I noticed that helping out further motivates and energizes me. So, I had started my journey as being the weight management coach and in no time with my passion of serving Muslim sisters, I acclaimed the title of "PCOS - weight management coach" and founded Be Fit – The Prophet's Way to help out Muslim sisters around the globe.

F: I want to talk about failure. You know obstacles and failures and challenges. When I look at people in my life that are close to me, I'm probably the person that has failed more than any other person I know. Tell us about failure and how pain has helped you grow.

N: God has blessed me with everything. I don't see myself going through big failure when I look at my life. My only struggle or pain was during my trials and error with my polycystic ovarian disease until I found the cure. Particularly the time when I would try experimenting with different foods to find the right diet for PCOS and couple of times my histamine would shoot up and I would have big hives on my skin and once ended up in the hospital emergency. This has helped me to understand what my clients go through and I can help them.

Overcoming weight issues and POCS make sisters more productive and they can make better decisions about their lives as well. Earlier they used to have brain fog with the unclear thought process. Clients who get pregnant, their husband's say that they like how their wives have transformed because sisters are more active and energetic even when pregnant.

The interesting part is when sisters would update their social media's profile photo after completing the program with a new version of them. They have a new strong mindset and their old social profile photo is not what they have become after joining and completing the program. This makes me feel content.

F: Nabillah what would say to your younger self?

N: I would say to that 16-year old that it is better for her to have faith in God and keep doing what is right and socialize a bit more because she used to be a book worm. I still enjoy reading books but now I also have friends with beautiful souls, who make each day beautiful.

F: Give us a little glimpse of the private Nabillah and what kinds of rituals and habits have you cultivated in your private life to make you the woman that you are today?

N: I try my best to follow the habits as our beloved Prophet as taught us from my childhood. I plan my day around the prayers. I would wake up at 4 am for prayer and special pray for my family and clients. I believe my service is incomplete without making pray for them. Then I would exercise, prepare breakfast, school lunches, etc. Get kids ready for school, by 7:45 am I head out the door to drop kids to school. From 9 am till 2:45 pm, I work with s 30 minutes break for prayer and lunch. I spend the evening with my family. We cook dinner together. After dinner at 6 pm, we go out for skating in winter or swimming in summer. After prayer, we are all asleep unless I have some work to do but max by 10 pm I would go to bed. 6- 7 hrs. Sleep is very significant for both wellbeing and productive day.

F: If there's somebody who's out there and they feel that they're gaining weight, they don't know wants to happen, they've got this acne issue. What is the best piece of advice and what do they need to do before they come and see you?

N: If someone has acne or weight loss that is not responding to any treatment out there, it means that something has gone out of balance within the body systems and it needs attention.

F: Nabilla how do people get in touch with you? What is the best way for people to get in touch with you? Online, Facebook, website, or phone number? How do they get a hold of you?

N: Sisters can book a session with me at www.pcosbreakthrough session.com and I can also be reached via the Facebook page, https://www.facebook.com/ PCOS Muslimism or Facebook group where sisters can share and talk about their PCOS in closed private environment
https://www.facebook.com/groups/MuslimahsandPCOS/

My email is nabillah@befitprophetsway.com

F: Any last-minute thoughts?

N: Lastly, I would like to say to all sisters out there having polycystic ovarian disease regardless of how long they have been battling with this symptom, how long they have been trying to conceive, my message to them is never lost hope, have faith in God and get the health support that makes sense for you.

"Take advantage of five matters before five other matters:

your youth, before you become old; your health before you fall sick; your richness, before you become poor; and your free time before you become busy; and your life, before your death."

Our bodies are a trust from God and will be asked on the Day of Judgment as to how did we use our bodies.

We keep our homes clean and beautiful similarly our soul resides in its home (that's our body) so why not learn and block some time to keep our body clean and healthy as well and stand feeling content on the day of judgment in front of God. Also, when we talk about someone not able to conceive, the question to ask is, do we know how to keep the baby home (uterus) healthy and in a baby-friendly environment?

We need to have a clear vision of what we want to down it hour health and have a clear direction where are we spending our clean earned money. If we can afford to spend on the internet and TV then why not invest in our health and we know this will not go to waste, unlike TV. Investing in a program that he plus overcome health issues for life is a win-win situation.

Also, we are never too busy when it comes to taking out time to care for our health.

ABOUT THE AUTHOR

Nabillah Farooq is the Founder and Coach at Be Fit – The Prophet's Way with Islamic medicine and allopathic medical background. She continues to study holistic and Islamic nutrition – based therapies to support and empower Frustrated stressed and over whelmed Muslim sisters, in particular, sister with PCOS (Polycystic Ovarian Syndrome) too overcome PCO through the language of food. Here sides in Canada with her lively four children.

Nabillah's passion to help Muslim sisters with PCO weight management began during her teen years. She went through her own tireless trial-and-error of overcoming PCOS until she found the answer in Islamic medicine. And as of now, with the will of God, she has helped numerous Muslim sisters around the globe to overcome their PCOS naturally and with the comfort of soothing pray from Holy Book and the best way. This has allowed sisters with PCOS to experience the joy of a healthy body and motherhood which in the past their Doctors had said, cannot happen.

Notes: ✍

NIDO ABDO

"The Astute Entrepreneur Focuses on a Scientific Approach to Growing Sales and Marketing Because They Understand It's How You Can Dramatically Increase Profits, Positioning, and Success"

Fatima: Welcome Nido. Please tell us about your business and the types of customers you help?

Nido: I own and operate a sales and marketing consulting business that specializes in helping companies that generate anywhere between $1 Million to $100 Million create structures and processes that attracts and converts more new clients

F: Tell us a little bit about back story. Did you come out of school saying "I want to work with a $100 Million company? Give us a little bit of the journey and what led you to this field.

N: I came to the US back in 1994 as a refugee after escaping a barbaric Civil War back in Somalia. At first, my dream has always been to become a professional soccer player. I played for a few teams growing up but when I realized professional soccer players weren't in my calling, I knew I had to find a plan B. I went to college and I tried a few different majors, tried different things and nothing seemed to click. Then somehow I fell in love with marketing so I would spend most of my days growing up going at a book store called Barnes and Noble.

While my friends were going out and having fun…I was studying sales and marketing inside of the book stores mainly because I wasn't able to afford to buy them at the time.

I studied for nearly a year straight and then Then I decided I was confident enough to start my consulting practice. I reached out to anyone who would listen to me…small business in my area, family and friends who owned businesses in the hopes of landing a deal. Looking back, I was even willing to work for food….I just needed someone to give me a shot.

But instead, most people laughed at me. They'd say things like, who does this kid think he is trying to tell us what to do. My family and friends would tell me to stay in school and focus on my studies. They didn't understand how hard I was working to become a sales and marketing expert

Needless to say, I didn't receive any requests for my services. However, I kept working at odd jobs, such as valet and a health club for minimum wage just to keep money coming in

After struggling for nearly 3 years, I finally got my big breakthrough in 2006 when I found a mentor, a very successful entrepreneur here in Massachusetts who was willing to give me a chance.

I offered to work for him for free for 6 weeks just so he could try me out and make sure that I can fulfill my duties.

What I told him was I might not have much of an experience or track record working as a marketing leader, but if you give me a chance, hiring me will be the best decision you'll ever make and he agreed. As they say the rest was history.

I was hired as the lead marketing strategist and even though I didn't have qualifications then, what got me the job was my hunger and passion to learn and succeed.

My Mentor, Dr. Tom trusted me to run his marketing department under my guidance, we were able to nearly double his revenue company.

This opportunity also came with some very unique perks. My mentor Dr. Tom believed in the importance of self-education so he belonged in a mastermind with some of the most elite entrepreneurs in the world. This mastermind got together 3 times a year and everyone in the group operated a seven-figure business. I was fortunate enough to go with him and get an insider's access to these amazing minds.

That's how I gained my knowledge. I was mentored by a very successful group of people and I showed up with an open mind and more importantly, I implemented what I learned.

F: Wow that's so amazing. What is the most common obstacle preventing a person from achieving amazing sales outcomes, branding themselves using marketing techniques that the big guys are using today in the online and offline world?

N: That's a very good question. One of the biggest obstacles I see that hold a lot of entrepreneurs back from achieving their maximum success is the fact that most entrepreneurs enter a field because they're either passionate about something. For example, someone might start a restaurant business because he or she is a good cook but the reality is if you don't know how to turn a business if you can't differentiate yourself from the other 20 restaurants just on your street….sooner or later your business will start to crumble.

Sadly, most business owners don't have marketing knowledge. You have these entrepreneurs that are focusing on product development, they're focusing on hiring people, and they're focusing on everything except for marketing. So that's one obstacle.

The second obstacle I see is for those that are doing marketing, they're launching big image marketing, big brand marketing, campaigns that companies like Nike and Apple often do but will never work for the small businessman.

I've seen too many hard-working entrepreneurs throw their money away by throwing their money at ineffective marketing campaigns. This is one of the main reasons 85% of businesses fail within the first 5 years

Want to know how small business owners can out-market their competition? Direct response marketing

Direct response marketing is simply having the ability to measure marketing as it goes out. For example, if you're spending $1,000 on marketing today with direct response marketing if you're doing it the right way and measuring every aspect of it, you know you're going to get back $2,000, $3,000, $5,000. And as long as you're doing that you will be on the right track.

F: So many people I speak to say they have this attitude where they say "why do I need to market? I'm a great dentist", "I'm a great architect", "I'm a great salesman and I don't need to market". What would you say to those people?

N: Yeah that's a very common thing that I hear. "I'm a great dentist so as soon as I open my practice people will beat a path to my door". But the reality is that people have choices, they have options, and if you can't answer the number one question that people have in their minds and it's not a question they will ask you directly and the question is "why should I come to you vs all the other options I have including the option of doing nothing?" If you can't answer that you're playing a dangerous game with your success as an entrepreneur. Unless you're able to distinguish yourself and one of the ways you can do that is not only having the right market system in place but having what's called a unique selling proposition.

So there needs to be something that as soon as your brand is mentioned, that you need to be able to come to the top of my awareness. So if you are not doing marketing in the right way and you're not able to differentiate yourself then you're not going to be able to succeed and especially successful in the long term.

F: Nido gives us some testimonials of the results that your clients have achieved.

N: Yeah I mean there are a lot of different examples that I can give you so I'll give you an old example and I'll give you a more recent example. One of the clients that I had had an event-based business so he was getting about 20 to 25 people to come to his workshops and he taught people how to become better accountants.

He was an accountant himself and one of the things that I realized he was doing wrong was he simply wasn't expressing his true persona to his market. Most of his marketing messages sounded like it came from a corporate company that wasn't congruent with what he was trying to convey.

Most business owners will do what I like to call one and done marketing. They might send you one postcard or one email or one direct mail in your mailbox and expect you to remember them. The reality is if you want to succeed you have to have a marketing campaign in place that's strategically designed to give value to your market.

Each marketing piece is created to bring your prospect one step closer to becoming a client. You might send an email accompanied by a phone call or a letter but basically, you are more strategic in your marketing. By simply deploying a very powerful marketing campaign for my client's business, what we were able to do is not only grow his business from having 20 to 25 people attend his events, we grew it to this year having almost 150 and we did almost $300,000 in sales. And this just kind of goes to show you that by simply deploying a marketing campaign vs. just doing a marketing one time and hoping people will come to you, there's a massive difference in place.

Another campaign that we worked on was we generated about $2.2 Million in a single weekend and again a lot of it was due to measuring every aspect of the marketing campaign we deployed

The secret was positioning and we had people from all over the world wanting to do business with us because we were the only solution in their minds. When you're able to position yourself as the best, you're able to demand premium prices. We nearly doubled his price. And the good news is because people now view you as the only option for them, they're not going to go price shopping, they're not going to bend your arm for a discount. They'll just buy it because they feel confident and comfortable working with you. At that campaign, we did $2.2 Million and the best part is we did it in just three days so that's the power of having a really powerful marketing campaign in place.

F: That's pretty impressive. Let me ask you something. When a client comes to you or your speaking to a potential prospect, is there some kind of a mindset change that they need to adapt to work with someone like you?

N: Absolutely. I turn down way more clients that I accept, especially in this stage of my business and the reason is a lot of people who come to me are very afraid of investing in marketing. They set aside a budget for almost everything else but they don't set a budget for the most important aspect of their business, which is marketing. So one of my questions to them is how much are you willing to spend on driving traffic? If the number is low or they're not comfortable answering this question - that shows me they don't get the value of marketing. Would you buy a beautiful car but then just leave it outside of your home because you don't want to put gas in it?

That's not different than working hard on business only to ignore marketing.

The good news is, in today's world there's a lot of different ways you can communicate with people. I only seek out clients who value marketing and are willing to spend on attracting people that they enjoy working with and are a perfect fit for their business

F: Were you always like this? Did you grow up in a family where you guys were big thinkers and you were thinking outside of the box and you were going to go conquer the world? Or was there some kind of evolution in your mind as a young Nido and then going to high school and getting married and working your way up? Give us that little bit of a journey and your private mind evolution.

N: There are three parts of my story. The first part was I was born in Somalia and we had a pretty decent life. My father had a good job with the government and we were doing okay. Then as you know the barbaric war started and we lost everything because we had to run for our lives. You go from living in a nice villa and pretty much having a decent life and then all of a sudden you're in a boat, running for your life, living in a refugee camp in Kenya. If that wasn't enough to turn your stomach, add starvation and sickness to the mix. God tests you in ways that only makes you stronger so I'm very much appreciative of that journey because I don't think I'd be half the man today without it.

This journey taught me probably the most important life lesson I got and that lesson was to not depend on anyone. When you're starving, you're sick and you're at the mercy of someone else at all times. You are scared, you are not home and basically, you become vulnerable and

I told myself I am never going to be in a position where I have to depend on other people, I just don't want to depend on someone else for me to live the kind of lifestyle that I want.

We were finally fortunate enough to get into the US as political asylum. I was already independent. The thing I enjoyed the most about America is that you can achieve anything you set your mind to. I know people love that as a slogan but it is true and the other thing was as I grew older, as I mentioned I wanted to be a professional soccer player, but when that didn't happen I was jumping from one thing to the next and the next. From the valet parking to the security guard and all these random jobs and I remember how some people would look at me as a failure. I would have all these intervention conversations with my family and some with friends and they would look at me kind of like someone who is going to be a bum and not do anything meaningful in his life (but I knew better). I knew this was part of the process. I knew in my heart-of-hearts that I would make something out of myself. To be honest with you it was just my motivation to prove people wrong that gave me the strength and the motivation I needed to pursue my dream

F: Thomas Edison said he didn't fail 10,000 times, he found 10,000 ways that didn't work and you have mentioned the fact that you guys escaped civil war and your soccer career didn't take off. Tell us how has failure and pain helped you to grow and become the man that you are today?

N: That's a great question. You know one of the things that I have learned early on is that everybody wants to be successful, everybody wants to achieve their goals whatever those goals might be. The reality is the reasons most people don't take the first step is that they are afraid of failure. I truly believe that the way the universe separates the people who want success and those who just want to talk about it is to see who is willing to fail and keep striving.

I was never afraid of failure, Even to this day there are a lot of things that I do that I am afraid to approach that right, a lot of new challenges that I take on that I don't know what the ending is going to look like but I still go for it because I know by me not even taking that first action I have already failed. I'm okay with failure I'm just not okay with never trying and I think this attitude developed a little bit from my sporting background where you have to be competitive.

You go into matches and sometimes you lose and you don't feel good about losing and you go home and you feel sad and it hurts but you know what? There's always that next game, right? And that's the same way in business. It's the same way with anything you are trying to achieve in life. You start your journey, you do your best, and if you fail there's always that next time. As long as you know that in the back of your mind, that failure is not the end but one obstacle, one way of life telling you "hey maybe there's a different thing you can try" you will eventually crack the code. Another way to look at it is if I give you a set of keys and I tell you to go to my house and open up the door and I give you a keychain that has 20 different keys. You might try the first one, you might try the second one or the third one and none of them open the door but you know eventually if you try all 20 keys one of them will open that door. Well, life is the same way. As long as you keep trying and trying and trying, eventually that door will be opened and that might be the door that's going to lead you to the best life that you have hoped for. But like I said most people don't take that first step and that's why a lot of people never live to see their dreams come to fruition.

F: Very true. What would you tell your younger self?

N: That everything will be okay. There are a lot of challenges that were coming and there was a big-time of my life where I was introvert. I didn't have that many friends in school. I was a shy kid and I got picked on a lot and so all these things were not very helpful to my confidence as you can imagine but I knew that every single thing that came my way was an obstacle for me to get better. I knew God wouldn't throw something at me to make me feel worse, I knew it was just a way to make me a stronger person and I would tell a younger Nido that all these things that you are going through right now, the lessons you are learning through adversity they will make you a better man as you grow older and I think that's true because today I live a life where I am very proud of it. I get to spend a lot of time with my kids, I get a lot of time with my wife, and I have a lot of really, really good friends who are very helpful and a lot of it came because of the journey and because I had a lot of pain with being a refugee and I had a lot of people disappoint me when I was young. I had people who made me promises that they didn't fulfill. I started with nothing, I remember not having much grown up and I appreciate all the things I have today because of the adversities. So yeah I would tell him hey man keep going because all these things are happening to you for a reason and in the end, it will turn out alright. And to probably clean his room.

F: The prophet [Peace Be upon Him] was a man of habits and rituals. Today we have Tony Robins who talks about rituals and habits that can break you and rituals and habits that can propel you into success. Give us a little glimpse into the private Nido and some of the rituals and habits that you have created in your life.

N: Yeah that's a very true statement. One of my favourite habits is that I am an early riser. No matter what time I sleep at night early, or late. I can go to bed at 3 am but I am usually up early, around 6 a.m., if I am super tired maybe 7. I do have my sweet four-year-old girl who wakes up that early most of the days to help me out but I do like to wake up early. The other habit I have is I like to read and I like to read because I feel that reading and learning from other people's experiences are part of the growth happening. It gives you massive shortcuts. I am not the kind of guy who sits and tries to figure things out on his own. I am always looking for ways to kind of gain an edge and I am always studying other experts and seeing what some of the top people in my field are doing so that I can take some of their efforts and apply to what I am doing. Another great habit I would say is getting the big rocks first. Right?

Every day I only have three big things that I am trying to get rid of. As long as I can get that done early in the day that kind of frees up the rest of my day. At the end of the day, I don't want to spend the whole time working. I have four kids and I make sure my schedule is around them and not the other way around. I love getting them ready for school, I love picking them up. My wife makes sure that we have a family dinner together so just having their day organized that way makes you feel better.

Anything that you do too much off, is probably not good for you. So waking up early, having the entire day organized and more importantly having your day organized the night before. This is a lesson that I learned over a decade ago, something Andrew Carnegie one of the first billionaires of the country used to do. He used to do six things only and he planned them the night before. You wake up ready to go. Those habits come in handy and helps you be more productive and more efficient.

F: Those are beautiful habits. Now let's get back to our client, the reader who picks up this book and they are looking for marketing sales advice. What would be some of the best pieces of advice you could give them before they consider contacting you?

N: First thing - understand the market. It doesn't matter what product you sell, it doesn't matter what business, whether you are a doctor, or a lawyer or an accountant. The first thing you have to understand is you are in the business of marketing your profession. You are not a dentist, you're in the business of marketing dentistry. You're not an accountant, you are in the business of marketing your accounting practice.

That's the mindset that you have to have. Every single thing that you do will be achieved to your maximum potential if you believe in the power of marketing. The second thing is that you have to understand that the goal of a business is getting a return on investment. That means don't do marketing to be cute.

If you watch the Super Bowl, some companies are spending $3-$4 Million for a 30-second spot just to be funny. It is ridiculous and I don't know how they get away with it but even if you are able to do that, some of those companies are billion-dollar companies but as a small businessman or small businesswoman you want to make sure that every single $1 you put into your practice or your business is returned $1, $2, $3 back and that's what I call direct response marketing.

There's a scientific way of figuring out whether your marketing is working or not working. The third thing is your willingness to follow advice. I shared my story with you in the beginning. I wouldn't be here today had it not been for the mentor, had it not been for the people who kind of showed me the way to becoming a better marketer. Today there are a lot of business people that I see who are struggling, who are barely able to keep their lights on, yet when you give them advice and you are giving those different strategies and different things they can try, they are still stuck on their old ways and they think they know better. They let their ego get in the way. I don't try to spend any time with those kinds of clients. As long as you are open to marketing and understand the value of marketing and direct response marketing and you're open to trying new approaches then I think we'll be able to have great conversations.

F: Great piece of advice. Nido if the reader wants to find out more information about you directly what is the best way online/offline that they can get a hold of you?

N: Yeah I mean first you can reach me at nidoabdo.com that's my main website and you can also shoot an email. Emails the best way that I respond, its nidoabdo@gmail.com and we can if it makes sense to have a conversation after that I'll be more than happy to chat with them. My main process and the way I help a lot of people is that they show me what they are doing or what their goals are and exactly what they should be doing and if they want to hire me to do it then we can have a further conversation. If they feel this is something they can handle internally great that's fine too. My main goal is to give people value so they can take the time we spend and at least get one or two ideas that they can implement immediately and instantly have it transform their business.

F: You are such a wealth of information. Any last thoughts?

N: I think you asked quite a bit of excellent questions. I truly appreciated that. If there's one thing I would add it is known that being an entrepreneur is not an easy thing. Everybody wants to be an entrepreneur or wants to become businessmen but not a lot of them do because it requires a certain type of personality to become successful. I want to encourage all entrepreneurs to listen to this and to understand your value to the world and how important you are.

> Entrepreneurs, you are the engine that runs our economy. When things get rough and hard it doesn't mean the end of the world. It just means time to try something different, try something new.

I wish you all the best and hope you got massive value from this chapter.

F: Thank you so much.

ABOUT THE AUTHOR

Nido is an author, international speaker, and considered a premier business coach that creates better business growth systems for both small and large businesses. He has significantly increased sales for his private clients who operate in more than 8 different industries by designing systems and processes that create new business opportunities, close more sales, and increase revenue.

Notes: ✍

Notes: ✍

MUHAMMAD NURUDDEEN LEMU

"Growth and contribution with compassion, wisdom, faith and fun" :)

Fatima: Welcome. Let's get right into it, who are the people that you help?

Nurudeen: I have been very fortunate to work with the Islamic Education Trust (IET) as Director for Research and Training of the Da'wah Institute of Nigeria (DIN), and tremendously blessed with a wonderful team of colleagues with whom I work. There are several things that we do there. One important thing we do at the DIN is that we conduct surveys to find out what trends, common misconceptions, questions, and issues about Islam and Muslims are on the rise among the Muslim youth in particular but also among the non-Muslims. We try to find out for example, what the most doubt-causing, faith-shaking and conscience-disturbing issues that are common among Muslims youths are. These are often also the indicators of irrational, unfair and unjust ideas that are being pedaled in the name of Islam within the Muslim community in particular by Muslims and non-Muslims. We also interview young Muslims and adults involved in the various forms of social and religious activism to identify knowledge and skill gaps we can help them with. We try to find out what are the issues contributing towards extremism or recruitment to radicalism, whether this is extremist attitudes towards women or against peaceful coexistence with people of other faiths, or extremism and animosity towards other

Muslims. We then research each issue identified to respond to them. Thereafter, we conduct "Train-the-Trainers" courses to further improve the capacities of local scholars, Imams, academics, preachers, activists, leaders of Islamic organizations, those involved in Inter-Faith work, etc. to more effectively tackle these real and on-the-ground issues that present various challenges in our communities and organizations. We have been blessed with a very good and diverse network of scholars advising and supporting us in this regard.

Our main mission at the Da'wah Institute of Nigeria (DIN) is the comprehensive capacity building of Islamic organizations and individuals involved in the Islamic enlightenment work to more effectively contribute towards greater social justice and peaceful coexistence within the community. Many of our activities focus on intra-faith and interfaith bridge-building and empowering others with the capacity for that. We put a lot of energy and time into building better relations between Muslim groups and helping them resolve many of the major sources of tension or conflicts between them and within the community.

At DIN, we conduct "Train-the-Trainers" courses, to empower the people that we train with the ability to train others. Thus, we don't deal with most members of the general public as a rule. Rather, we try to focus more on the people that deal with the general public. This, we believe, is more efficient, faster, and so far more effective and impactful. We just build the capacity of others to do more of what they're already doing but with better skills and methods, more knowledge, and better reasons for respecting our diversity. Our training programs and courses cover a wide range of topics such as interfaith relations and peaceful coexistence, gender equity, Islamic jurisprudence, and critical thinking, da'wah resource management, personal development and leadership, ethical and moral development, countering violent extremism and several other topics related to misconceptions about Islam. We have so far conducted our courses in nearly 20 countries on all continents.

F: Tell us a little bit of your journey. Who inspired you? Was it your parents? What was the journey that led you to this field?

N: I believe of course that God is behind everything. However, I think that as with most people, my parents, and social environment have been the most critical influences in my life. My mother was a convert to Islam in the '60s. She had moved from Christianity to Hinduism, dabbled in Buddhism, dabbled in this and that and finally became a Muslim. That was useful to me as she had answers to a lot of the questions of why this belief and why not that. At home, there were so many books on different religions, thus interest in interfaith issues was not a strange thing. My mum's side of the family was also Christian, but her father, my grandpa became more Agnostic after the Second World War. He was a Major in the British Army during the war and was very much affected and disillusioned by what he experienced. He never liked to talk about it. I did, however, get to have a few interesting discussions with him about God, human nature, and religion before he passed away while I was doing my Master's degree in Scotland. I should also say that some of my extended family members were/are non-Muslims and I believe that it did help with more exposure to people of other faiths that I was close to. I, therefore, wasn't religiously isolated in that sense even though I live in a Muslim-majority environment.

Before and after embracing Islam while at the University of London, my mother took her study of Islam very seriously. She wrote books and textbooks about Islam that are being used for Islamic studies in secondary schools in several countries. She gave talks about Islam all over the world, and along with some of her friends set up various Islamic organizations. My dad was, until he retired, a Grand Khadi, which is like the chief judge of the Shari'ah Court of Appeal in Minna where we still live. So he had a deep understanding of traditional

Islamic scholarships and the Islamic sciences. That I think also influenced the quality of knowledge in the environment I grew up with. My parents had together with some of their friends and colleagues set up an Islamic organization – the Islamic Education Trust - so there were always programs going on especially during holidays that my siblings and I would have to help in supporting in whatever way we could. Through this interaction, I got to meet some of their friends, and many other wonderful people of similar interests.

When I went to secondary school, I became a member of the MSSN - the Muslim Student Society of Nigeria – and was nominated to be the president. I think because of who my parents were and how well known they were, there was also this expectation that I was supposed to have answers to various questions about Islam. If fellow students couldn't answer some questions, it was expected that I should be able to answer, or at least know where to get the answers from. That I believe put an indirect burden on me to learn more about Islam, and fortunately, the resources and experts were either at home or not too far away. So I think that my environment helped me in major ways, and I'm grateful to God for that. The opportunity to hold various positions within the Muslim Students' Society also gave me heaps of practice in public speaking and in polishing my presentation skills.

Also, within the secondary school and university environment in Nigeria, there was a strong competitive Muslim and Christian presence, and also a strong Evangelical movement even in my secondary school – the Federal Government College Minna. This coincided with a time when people like the late Ahmed Deedat from South Africa came onto the world scene to confront Christian evangelism and defend it from especially Christian polemics against Islam. We found a lot of his resources useful in defending ourselves from the advances of evangelists and critics. Of course, at that time it wasn't inter-faith dialogue, but was termed "Comparative Religion". In reality, it was more about the debate, more to win the argument even if you lose the heart of a friend. It was about defeating the other person and protecting the dignity of your religious identity. It, unfortunately, had little to do with developing mutual understanding and respect for each other. I guess as teenagers who felt their faith and religious pride was under attack, defense and counter-attack was a natural response. All these experiences contributed to many ways of steering me in the direction I presently find myself.

F: Mm-hmm.

N: With age and experience, I think it became clearer that that approach was probably not the best way of growing in my understanding of others or sharing Islam better. Nearly all relationships I know that took that path eventually degenerated or even died. If all you do is attack another person's cherished beliefs without curiously listening to or trying to understand them, then they will also attack back and not listen to try to understand you. Such an approach often starts a chain reaction of polemics and argument that simply puts your ego ahead of the objectives of your faith – better mutual understanding and respect for each other's faith. It is left to the conscience of the individual to decide what to do with a better understanding of the other. The Holy Book statement that "there is no compulsion in religion" was not sufficiently digested by many of us at that time.

However, while all that was going on, we realized that there were so many misconceptions that Muslims and non-Muslims have about Islam, and as we started tackling and answering those misconceptions, we started recognizing how many Muslims didn't know the answers to some of those basic questions asked by non-Muslims. Meanwhile, as we started organizing training and classes to help Muslims respond to difficult questions, we met other Muslims who began arguing with us and trying to discredit our answers and the opinions we were sharing. That challenge took us into trying to understand the differences of opinions among past and present Muslims scholars on various topics. So while the journey early on went in the general direction of explaining Islam to others, it gradually started turning around and inwards, and looking more closely at Islam and how Muslims understand and live it.

The other challenge with the focus on intra-faith relations was discovering and encountering young Muslim extremists (as we preferred to identify them by) who only compounded the simple and straightforward understanding or presentation of various aspects of Islam for many people. If we were going to have more people sharing Islam with others, we would need to do a lot more with the diversity within the "rooms" that are within the "house of Islam".

While all that was going on, it became clearer over the years that too many people were being killed in conflicts between Muslims and Christians in the name of their respective faiths, even if at the root of it, religion was not the issue. Sometimes it was ethnicity - who was an indigene and who was a settler/migrant – sometimes it was over political parties and perceptions of power and control over resources, but somehow there was always a religious dimension to it which was difficult to understand and justify. Living according to one's faith is a religious option that should not on its cause a problem. If Muslims and Christians on campuses, in the markets and all over the place were living in relative peace with each other, what exactly was it that resulted in repeated violence in certain locations? Muslims generally blame it on Christian/Western hatred for Islam and Muslims, and Christians feel the same about us.

We knew many active faithful and peace-loving Christians, but have also seen, especially on the media very bigoted, spiteful and hate-driven Christians who could make any normal Muslim's blood boil over in anger. But we have also seen and met Muslims who were just as bad. Each seemed to be the proof and justification for the other, and each claimed to speak for their community. Nearly every conversation about Islam and Christianity in Nigeria would turn and end with a focus on violence and an argument on who was more violent than the other in history. It was and still is very messy. We in time began to appreciate more the mutual respect and peace-building potentials of interfaith dialogues and the activities of those involved in such discussions. There was the need to start looking at interfaith relationship-building between religious people who cared for peaceful coexistence from both sides of the religious divide. As we attended more interfaith dialogues and events, we got to know many more broad-minded cosmopolitan people of various faiths. That exposure has helped me become a bit more humble, curious and committed to intra-faith and interfaith peace building. I see Nigerian Muslims and Christians now as all in a big "boat" called Nigeria but which is threatened by the corrupt and extremist individuals claiming to belong to and speak for each faith. The challenge I believe is for people of good faith in each religion to each tackle their respective intra-faith extremists and hot-heads, while together facing the many mutually challenging problems of a developing nation like Nigeria.

While I have benefitted from numerous scholars and authors over the years, some of the early books and presentations by Muslim scholars that served as a turning point for me were by people such as Isma'il al-Faruqi, Khurram Murad, Jamal Badawi, and Jeffrey Lang, among many others of course. I continue to pray for God blessings on them.

Over the last decade or so and with the rise of religious and other forms of extremism in many places, my colleagues and I have been spending more time in developing better ways of building resilience within the community against various forms and expressions of religious extremism. We have been helping more people with better critical thinking skills derived from the classical tools of Islamic jurisprudence that allow them to more easily identify and systematically critique extremist, unjust and harmful opinions related to relations with non-Muslims, women's rights, Islamic law, and a host of other issues. We train religious activists, Imams and laypeople in a course we call "Shari'ah Intelligence" which is a carefully developed purpose-driven introduction to the principles of Islamic jurisprudence (Usul al-Fiqh) and the higher intents and purposes of Islam (Maqasid al-Shari'ah). It is one of the most powerful antidotes and cures of religious extremism for Muslims that I have come across so far, and I'm very excited about the results so far especially in Nigeria, Malaysia, and Australia.

F: I want to get into the crux of the problem, the core of this chapter for you. You've got Muslims, you've got inter-faith, intra-faith and all the confusion around that. What do you think is the biggest misconception that we are having these days? The obstacle that prevents us from achieving happy homes, happy lives? Is it people of different faiths or different sects of Islam?

N: That's a million-dollar question, and I'm probably too young and limited in my perspectives to answer that correctly. However, I do think we (or maybe I) unfortunately don't have one answer to that question because when we look at the current rise of different types of extremism everywhere, it's difficult to simplify and isolate the cause of the problem or the solution. We have extremism on the Right and Left, Xenophobic, Racist, Buddhist, Muslim, Christian and Atheistic extremisms. With all the social, economic, political and educational advancements of some societies, many seem not to have been able to graduate from basic primitive racism, bigotry, and discrimination. This is very disturbing because it would otherwise have simply been a problem of poverty, political freedom, and educational backwardness, etc. While each of these is important and has its many benefits, the challenges appear to be more complex than we think. I believe there is a place for more to be done in the area of ethical peace-building and conflict management if the world is only expected to get more globalized, pluralized and crowded. For the Muslim peoples, I believe the obvious and greatest challenge presently facing Muslims is violent extremism that is carried out in the name of Islam by some Muslims and mostly against other Muslims.

The Prophet said that a reformer (reformer) would appear every century to raise his public from its decay; to re-present Islam anew to Muslims and revive the Islamic spirit of compassion, justice, wisdom and the common good for all. The need for a reformer automatically implies the existence of periodic decay. I believe it is obvious that we are currently in a state of intellectual and moral decay and I do not see the benefit in denying this. To claim everything is okay with his publics and the problem is all out there is, I believe, only to our peril and to delay the necessary reforms we need to make to how we think about and view Islam. Islam for many Muslims is unfortunately like a compass that has lost its polarity and they find it difficult to know what to do once they hear there is a difference of opinion among scholars on an issue – as there will always be.

At the core of this decay is I believe the decline in the poor quality and quantity of good juristic reasoning by many of our scholars. The fact appears to be that competent scholars of Usul al-Fiqh (the Principles of Islamic Jurisprudence) and Maqasid al-Shariah (the higher objectives and purposes of Islamic law) have become like an endangered species. The quantity of irrelevant and poor quality or even detrimental Islamic law on many important issues is only matched by or coupled with the inability of most lay Muslims to distinguish a competent jurist or good religious answer (or Islamic law) for their context from one that is not appropriate. This I find very disturbing. It very often resembles a situation where patients who go to a hospital where the nurses and lab technicians, rather than doctors, are giving prescriptions to patients. But to make matters worse, the patients appear to not be able to distinguish a doctor from a nurse, or a dentist from a gynaecologist or psychiatrist. The patients seem to regard every staff in the hospital who is wearing a white coat or uniform as a competent doctor. Also, anyone called "doctor" is regarded by the more educated laypersons as someone who is a specialist at handling every illness! The relationship between Muslims and the different specialist scholars is regretfully very similar to this.

One of my favourite quotes related to Islamic jurisprudence is one by the distinguished jurist, Bin Qayyim al-Jawziyyah where he says, "The foundation of the Shari'ah is wisdom and the safeguarding of people's welfare in this life and the next. In its entirety, it is about justice, mercy, wisdom, and good. Every rule which replaces justice with injustice, mercy with its opposite, the common good with mischief, and wisdom with folly, is a ruling that does not belong to the Shari'ah, even though it might have been claimed to be according to some interpretation..." I in all humility regard this as one of the most profound summaries so far of what Shari'ah is all about. I honestly believe that anyone who would like to dismiss this statement as too simplistic needs a good dose of "Shari'ah Intelligence" – the Principles and Objectives of Islamic Jurisprudence. So many Muslims say they want more of Shari'ah guiding and governing their lives. Yet most Muslims I have met can't even write a single page on what the actual objectives (purposes) of Shari'ah are and how those ends and purposes governor regulate the processes of making and applying of Shari'ah rulings. And you'd think that studying the aims and objectives of something would be the first thing to know about a subject, system or way of life! However, because many Muslims want more Shari'ah, it easily becomes a bait to lure some Shari'ah-loving Muslims into doing the most unimaginable atrocities in the name of Shari'ah. Yet, many more don't want to have anything to do with Shari'ah primarily because of the amount of injustice, cruelty, folly and harm that some of our 'pious' brothers and sisters present as Shari'ah; teachings that have very little to do with the higher intents and values-oriented reform that Islam proposes for society.

Unless Muslims community leaders, da'wah workers, scholars, speakers and those who invite them get acquainted with the most fundamental principles and objectives of Islamic jurisprudence, and the different specialists and competencies within the Islamic Sciences, the Muslim Peoples will not have any filters against its own folly, let alone make constructive contributions to society that will always be in line with justice, mercy, wisdom and the common good. I honestly believe that an introduction to the field of Usul al-Fiqh and Maqasid al-Shari'ah by a competent scholar is today an "Individual Obligation" (Fardu's law) for anyone who wants to speak publically about or on behalf of Islam in these confusing times. Fortunately, these disciplines are gradually becoming more popular in some circles and a few good books on them are available in English. But I believe a lot more still needs to be done to empower lay Muslims with these filters against folly and the basic tools of sensible faith-based critical thinking about interpretations of the Holy Book and the best way for a particular context. It is in this vein that we are trying to popularize "Shari'ah Intelligence". Of course, the challenges are more than just this, but I think this is one of the most important starting points for any Muslim, to learn to think sensibly about Islamic issues. This is also something distinguished jurists and scholars such as Sheikh Abdullah bin Bayyah and several others have been trying to do for some time now.

Without trying to be too simplistic about possible starting points for improving our intellectual situation, I would also like to highly recommend as a starting point five important principles shared by another distinguished American scholar of Usul al-Fiqh, Sheikh Dr. Umar Faruq Abd-God in his paper Living Islam with Purpose. To make it more memorable, we at the Da'wah Institute teach these five principles with the acronym "TREES". The five are 1. The trusting reason; 2. Respecting dissent and differences; 3. Embracing the legal maxims; 4. Emphasizing social obligations; and 5. Setting priorities. I cannot summarize his paper here, but would very highly recommend it as one of the best structured operational frameworks for understanding presenting Islam in contemporary society to especially Muslims, but also non-Muslims.

Abu Hamid al-Ghazali once said that the relationship between good reasoning and revelation was similar to the relationship between the eyes and light. To try and follow good reasoning without revelation was similar to trying to find one's way in the dark with your eyes wide open. To follow revelation without good reasoning he said, was similar to trying to move around in broad daylight with one's eyes shut. Both the eyes and lights are gifts from God to guide us and they must both be used. Similarly, both good reasoning and revelation are gifts from God to guide us in this world towards the hereafter.

So in response to your question about what I believe may be the biggest misconception about Islam from among Muslims, it is I believe, that many Muslims think that good sound reasoning has little or nothing to do with following the Holy Book and best way; that it is one or the other instead of a healthy mix of the two. On the contrary, God describes the message of the Holy Book as being "for those who think" (li easy-to-use) and one of the unanimously accepted fundamental objectives (purpose) of Shari'ah is the promotion and preservation of the intellect (hifzul 'intellect). As Sheikh Umar Faruq Abd-Allah once said, "Islam must make sense, but, to make sense, it requires intelligent followers with sound understanding".

But having said all that, and while the intellectual reform is important, our character and the condition of the heart is ultimately the most critical for any human being's destiny before God. For improving our moral and ethical compass, a lot is going on in many places but much more is needed for our character and ethical reformation. I believe the work being done by Fons Vitae, Shaykh Hamza Yusuf and others on the Ghazali Children's Project has tremendous potential to bring better humanity and the true compassionate spirit of Islam into our younger ones and the next leadership of tomorrow.

I honestly don't have a simpler answer than this to your last question. And God knows best.

ABOUT THE AUTHOR

Mr. Muhammad Nuruddeen Lemu is the Director of Research and Training at the Da'wah Institute of Nigeria (DIN), Islamic Education Trust (IET) in Minna, Nigeria. He develops, facilitates and conducts train-the-trainers courses in enhancing inter-faith dialogue and engagement, intra-faith cooperation, responding to various forms of religious extremism among Muslims, and promoting faith-based critical thinking ("Shari'ah Intelligence").

He is a Director of several organizations including Lotus Capital (permissible Investments) Limited, the Development Initiative of West Africa (DIWA), and a co-founder of the Inter-Faith Activity and Partnership for Peace (IFAPP). He holds various positions on many other organizations that focus on issues related to social welfare, government policy, education, sustainable development, environment, leadership, family life, youth empowerment, and gender equity.

Mr. Lemu has trained and given talks to students, lecturers, youth and community leaders in over 20 countries, and he has moderated, presented and produced more than two hundred radio and television programs. Nearly half of these have been on interfaith bridge-building and engagement (the IFAPP's "Inter-Faith Forum") aired on the African International Television (AIT) and Ray Power Radio. He was also nominated by the Nigeria Supreme Council for Islamic Affairs (NSCIA) to represent the Nigerian Muslim Leadership at the National Conference (CONFAB 2014).

Lemu is a Fellow of the Africa Leadership Initiative of West Africa (ALIWA), and the Aspen Leadership Institute, Aspen, Colorado, USA. He holds a MSc. in Resource Management from Edinburgh University, the UK, and a bachelor's degree in Agriculture from Ahmadu Bello University, Zaria, Nigeria.

His motto is "Growth and contribution with compassion, wisdom, faith, and fun".

Notes:

RAYDA EDDING

"Women can have it all"

Rayda Edding, also lovingly known as Umm Mohamed, a mother, a wife, an investor who has successfully raised 6 beautiful children, happily married, and created multiple businesses in her lifetime and still able to create balance in her life.

Conversation with Rayda Edding

Fatima: Can you tell us a little about what you do and the kind of businesses you deal with and who you are?

Rayda: I came to America in 1989 as a student, coming from a very poor city in The Philippines. Coming here penniless, my only calculator was my brain of course. I had several scholarships and when I came here I was getting my P.H.D in genetic engineering. After less than a year, while I was getting my P.H.D I met my husband. I was very career-oriented and I was just eager to get my goals.

Thank God, I met my husband and got married. He said: "I love your goals and I love the plans you're making but you're not doing business with God? Because you have forgotten about your prayer and fast!"

That hit me. This man was making sense. I was so driven to reach all my goals, that were all world related.

I told myself I need to learn the Quran again. I did not understand Islam. I was also doing engineering, and I was exposed to a lot of radioactive materials. At that time in 1987, we were not protected against radioactive materials and for some reason, I kept having miscarriages. After I had my first child, I decided I want to be a stay at home mom, and spend my time with my children.

I saw a lot of contradictions with women. Either, you're a very successful person, and your children are left behind or the other way around.

For me, I made the conscious decision to be successful in both my personal life and business life. My priority at that time was to be a wife first, then a mom and then a business owner. My husband was relieved that I decided to stay home, after being active in so many things and doing so many jobs.

After that, he bought a business for $900 and told me to run it. From $900 it grew to $1 million. We sold it for $250,000. After that, we bought our house with cash.

We went into different businesses. We went into real-estate and we did some online businesses. Also a brick and mortar business and restaurants.

With six children I can proudly say I was with them every single day, change their diapers. They have never been to any daycare. I was the one who took care of them. I can vouch to this day they have seen my values Alhamdulillah.

F: What do you think are your biggest achievements, besides your lovely children?

R: My biggest achievement is that I was able to raise my family and run a successful business at the same time from the comfort of my home.

Whenever my family needed me I was always there. That's one of my biggest achievements and I owe it all to God.

F: Can you tell us a little bit more about the businesses that you and your husband have grown together?

R: I had different businesses at different stages of our lives. At first, I had three different businesses in the three major stages of my life.

The first stage was when I was pregnant I was taking care of really small children, God blessed us where I could do it at home. It was a kitchen-run business. I would do all the marketing and I would do all of the customer's service just by using the phone. I would advertise and people would call me and inquire about the products. It was home placement meals for:

- People who want to lose weight,

- People who have medically restricted diets,

- Low-fat meals,

- Low sodium meals,

- And protein meals.

I would buy it from a company that produced everything. I would market it to people who want to continue having healthy food in their homes.

I was the middle man.

When my husband bought the business for $900. With only 4 customers, I was able to build it to several hundred. In a week, if you have a hundred customers, that's about $5,000. That is profit. I was always making phone calls and changing diapers at the same time.

In the next 10 years, we started to flip houses and flip apartment buildings. My husband and I would go and check what needs to be done. We did the construction work because we did everything ourselves. That's one of the reasons I think we are well off financially. My husband knows how to handle the money. For him, once the money gets into his hands there's no way it's getting out. With that kind of financial habits, we were able to save a lot.

We live very simply but we think big.

Now, I have more freedom because my youngest is 13 years old and my oldest is 24 years old. I can be out most of the time and deal with the workload.

Then we went into the restaurant business. A middle-eastern restaurant, where I can be there monitoring the workers and make sure it runs smoothly. I was very hands-on at this stage in our business.

Our, children who were given early exposure in the business are now our partners in the business. They are driven by the same passion to succeed in business. Different businesses in different stages of our lives were a big blessing.

F: What do you think is the biggest pitfall and the common obstacles for mothers that are holding them back from achieving the kind of success you have?

R: It's a very big misconception. Women think either I do my Afterlife or I do the world. They feel they need to choose whether my family or my career. I think if I was advising my younger self or a younger woman out there, I would say always put it as a priority. Tell yourself whatever I am doing; I am doing it for the sake of God. That is always my mantra. I was always telling myself and everything that I do now; I am doing seeking the pleasure of God alone.

There are times for example that I am in the house taking care of the young children and there are times I hardly see my husband him because he has a job in the hospital doing research. At some point, you get frustrated and disappointed like I am not getting any help.

Then I go back to the main goal, I am doing this for the sake of God. I don't get any help and it doesn't matter because I am not doing this to make my husband happy or for him to tell me that I am doing a good job. Even if I didn't get that, I was moving on. I think it's very important to tell ourselves that.

Whatever we do it's to seek the pleasure of God and when you do that God puts everything in perspective.

I just felt like I was moving on with my life and the best thing on my end. Sometimes you'll say, nobody's helping me and I am so frustrated here but you know what? God going to reward me. If you go with the mentality and in my case, everything just fell into perspective. The purpose of that perspective was fully manifested. It just got easier and easier. It's different now. Women think I have to do this and do that to support the family and doing this. I know with myself if it's so much. So I think we need to change this and by changing that everything will be better.

F: Thank you for your time. What an enlightening conversation. How can we get in touch with you?

R: My Facebook page

F: Thank you for your time.

R: Welcome

ABOUT THE AUTHOR

Rayda Edding, also known as Umm Mohammad, is a fulltime mother of 6, wife, Businesswoman (Restaurateur - Real Estate Investor and E-commerce), Student of Knowledge, World Traveler, and Humanitarian Worker. When not busy with her family and businesses, Sr. Rayda attend to several of her non-profit organizations which are supported by her businesses. Being a student of Knowledge, Sr. Rayda is also actively involved in Dawah work and Islamic Education. Very adventurous and having traveled to more than 56 countries, Sr. Rayda plans to become a global citizen and fulfill her dream to live in different parts of the world.

Facebook
Facebook.com/Rayda.Edding

Notes:

SHOMAIL MALIK

"Conceived To Be A Doctor"

Shomail Malik is an entrepreneur, a trainer, and a real estate investor. He offers multiple avenues for investors to invest in permissible real-estate so they can feel good about their money, they can make a difference and get rich.

Conversation with Shomail Malik

Fatima: Welcome, Shomail!

Shomail: Sister Fatima. It's a pleasure to be here.

F: Shomail tells us about your business. What type of customers do you help and what do you do?

S: I run a private real-estate investment firm and what we essentially do is we offer an avenue for investors to safely invest in real estate. You don't have to be Muslim to invest with us and we do have many non-Muslim investors as well. We provide a unique platform for working professionals and folks who want to put their money to work in a clean investment vehicle to invest in turn-key income properties as well as our fix-and-flip rehab projects. We interface with a lot of physicians, IT consultants, corporate executives, and the like that are constantly searching for ways to put their money to work. Interestingly enough, the Muslim community happens to be the second most affluent demographic in the United States. So we have done well for ourselves, however, what I find more often than not is that a lot of people are not financially literate as far as how to invest their money Permissible investment vehicle to invest in turn-key income properties as well as our fix-and-flip rehab projects. We interface with a lot of physicians, IT consultants, corporate executives, and the like that are constantly searching for ways to put their money to work. Interestingly enough, the Muslim community happens to be the second most affluent demographic in the United States. So we have done well for ourselves, however, what I find more often than not is that a lot of people are not financially literate as far as how to invest their money.

That's where we come in and provide advisory and consultative services and show them how to park their money into real estate so that they can grow their wealth without having to worry about being a landlord or actively managing their portfolio. We will educate them on the entire process, explain to them how the numbers work, and hold their hands throughout the entire process.

I started the company about 8 years ago and we now have about 9 employees and we do millions of dollars in revenue each year. The majority of our business is in New Jersey and we also have operations in Ohio, Michigan, and Maryland.

F: that sounds wonderful. Give us a little bit about your back-story. Did you just get out of school and get into real-estate? What was the journey that led you to the journey of what you are doing today?

S: Not at all. I always joke that my parents conceived me to be a doctor. That is typically the option that you are given if you are a Pakistani or from the Indian Sub-continent. It is either a doctor or an engineer. My parents came over to the United States with a dream that their first-born was going to do the family proud and go into medicine. That was drilled into my head as far as early as I can remember and when I went into college, I pursued a major in Cell Biology & Neuroscience. That sort of changed in college when I got involved in the network marketing business. I was doing extremely well financially while still in college and making more than my dad at a certain time. After a few months, that company went belly-up but it created a lasting change within me as far as my interests to pursue medicine as a career path. I didn't want to go through 4 years of medical school after college, then another three years of residency and then finally make my first penny, while potentially being in debt from having loans from medical school, I wanted to come out with guns blazing right after school and start making money. Just before graduating college, I also got involved in real-estate through one of my contacts and became a real estate agent for Keller Williams and where I met Mr. Mohammad Abbasi, who would mentor me and teach me the ropes of the business. It wasn't just real estate principles that I've come to learn from him. Business principles, how to structure my day to day routine, discipline myself through habit and time-blocking, and all of these elements became critical as I started to taste success in my field.

Anyway, when I came out of college I was still working in real estate but it was a commission-based job, and I was getting engaged to be married. I couldn't go to my father in law and say, "Hey one month I am going to close a deal and eat fancy lobster dinner, but the next month we might starve." So I enlisted into the rat-race and joined corporate America as a pharmaceutical sales rep. It was a cushy job at Fortune 500 Company that started me out around $65,000 a year, provided a company car, an AMEX Corporate card and got to eat out at fancy 5-star restaurants. I wasn't there too long, as I found myself working for other pharma companies soon after but the position and responsibilities were relatively the same.

The best part was – I was good at it. Over those 11 and half years that I worked in healthcare sales, I won trips to Hawaii, tons of sales awards, and promotions that put me in the seat of the Global Business Manager managing a $35M business unit. It was a copious amount of responsibility for a young man of 31, and it kept me busy. My daily commute consisted of anywhere between 2 to 4 flights every day, flying from city to city all over the United States. I would wake up in New Jersey, have lunch in Tennessee, and made it in time for a business event in Ohio for dinner. The worst part was that I was away from my wife and kids for 3-4 days of the week. There was no way I was going to do this forever.

While in Corporate America, because my work was mostly field-based and I was rarely ever in an office, I had more autonomy and free time than I knew what to do with. So to capture it and make use of it all, I made the move back into real estate investing in 2008. Back then we were buying the properties for about 20 to 60 cents on the dollar and then we would turn around and flip it the same day and profit $30,000 to $40,000. Sometimes even more within an hour to 2 hour time period, and doing 5 or 6 of those a year along with my job was incredibly rewarding. Life was good. We were making 6 figures, I had started my executive MBA in 2010, and had my first child along the way, all within the 2 years between 2008 and 2010. Fast forward another couple of years to 2012 and I started to get serious with my real estate business and take it to the next level. I went into the community to say, "Hey who wants to invest with me on our projects and profit with me?" It was time to scale up and share with the public my success in the field and build something bigger.

After capturing the community's interests I worked to captivate their imagination as to what was possible in the world of real estate, raising about $20 million. When I told you that we have very, very wealthy individuals in our community, it's true. I met with a brother yesterday together with his cousins and his father in law and they are looking to invest about $3 million. I wanted to be the go-to person when people are thinking "I have all this money that I want to invest, but don't know where to safely invest and still have exceptional returns," and that is what the company has evolved into overtime. With offices in

New York and New Jersey, plus operators and representatives in New Jersey, Ohio, Michigan, and Maryland, we are expanding throughout the United States. Soon we will be in every U.S. market where it would make sense to invest in real estate and real estate rentals. To accomplish this I've surrounded myself with A-list team members that work around the clock towards our goals. We have got many full-time people and a few part-time and we continue to grow.

F: What a beautiful journey! What advice would you give people who are thinking about investing in real estate but don't have any idea where to start? Also, what are some obstacles that prevent some people from investing?

S: It's generally the knowledge, education, and time. So many people that are making good money are typically putting in hour after hour in their primary occupations, and for that reason, they don't have a lot of time to run another business successfully. What they can do instead, is leverage somebody that's already in the business and take advantage of that person's time and expertise and invest passively with them. Also, there are a lot of myths and urban legends tales about rental properties; that if one becomes a landlord, they would have to deal with the entire headache that comes along with it. After all, who wants the call in the middle of the night that the toilet is clogged, or the furnace isn't working, or the light just went out? If you are working with a company and all of that grunt work is done for you, then you don't have to do any of that. Unfortunately, some people are either not informed that there are things such as a property management company to handle these issues.

A lot of you reading this book that is finding out about it for the first time now have this knowledge that such companies exist, and can potentially set you on the path to financial freedom through passive investments. I encourage you to Google rental turn-key providers and read up more on how all of this works. We are one of these rental turn-key providers and have been very successful in that space. It's all about knowledge and time. If it's internet marketing, if it's selling apps, whatever it is; do I know, and if not, do I have the time to learn it and apply that knowledge? If your answer to those questions is "no", partnering with one of these turn-key providers is a way to bypass that and partner with somebody who has that knowledge and experience. They gain a fruitful partner, you begin to acquire the knowledge and learn about that field while benefiting from it. It's a collaboration that results in a win-win for both parties involved, and that's what doing business is all about.

F: Yeah, that's awesome. That's a really good synopsis. What happens with people who don't have a lot of money? Is there a minimum investment with your clients that you recommend?

S: I'll be very straight-forward about addressing this point. Typically minimum investments for these properties are about $70,000 to $95,000. Some markets offer properties for that amount of money if you have a higher risk appetite. If people are open to the idea of Islamic financing we can work something out in a more secure neighbourhood for that same amount, but the community's opinion, quite frankly, is split on Islamic financing. Some people think it's the viable option and others think it's no different than conventional financing and interest is involved. We leave it to the people to do their due diligence and see what the scholars they follow have to say about that and which positions they feel comfortable taking.

For example, if it's a $60,000 property, you don't have to come with $60,000 from your pocket. You can go to a bank like University Islamic Financial or Guidance Residential. They are two of the most prominent Islamic banks to offer this financing service in North America. If you are willing to put up 20-25% of the purchase price, as most companies require this amount of down payment upfront, that's about a $12-15,000 investment. They will give you a mortgage and you can use this sort of financing to acquire the property. Of course, you will have a mortgage to pay every month but it's your tenant that is going to be paying the mortgage through their rent. Another option that you have in your tool belt if you only have $10,000 is to go find a cousin or a brother or maybe a parent that has $10,000, and find three or four people in your family and friends and pull the money together. Put your money together and start a company, an LLC. Put that money into the company and once that happens, that company can buy a property to benefit all members of the company.

Profit shares will be dependent on contribution. If $1,000 came in every month, and you and your cousin split the acquisition cost fifty-fifty, then you both made $500 respectively. You don't have to have the money yourself, but you need to be able to have access to the money. In real estate it's not about having resources but more about being resourceful. You can connect people. Pull your funds together then invest it to make something work with benefactors. The opportunity is out there, you just have to chase it.

The third way and a lot of people don't know about this because it's probably one of the best-kept secrets in the financial world, is you can use your 401K retirement plan and IRA to invest in real estate. Most of the people that I meet got married at a young age and have kids. They send their kids to private schools, have tuition, rents, mortgages, and groceries to pay for so by the end of the month, they can't save a lot of money. However, they are contributing to a 401K plan that has been cutting from their pay check every month. Some company is even contributing dollar for dollar or they are doing some sort of match program with the 401K. And even when you leave that company for whatever reason life throws at you, it's possible to take that money and roll that over into a self-directed individual retirement account or as it's more commonly referred to as a self-directed IRA. Then you can do exactly what the name suggests, you can direct that investment into real estate. What I find more often than not is people don't have much money in their checking and bank account, but they have a significant amount of money because they have been putting money away from their 401K for years. Instead of investing it into traditional stock and business funds, most don't know that you can self-direct that and own property through that IRA.

Those are three different out-of-the-box solutions that somebody can employ to be able to own real estate if they don't have a lot of money, and are all very feasible, practical solutions.

F: Brilliant. Shomail, I want to ask you about your mindset. There's a certain type of belief system and attitude to create success. What do you think makes you different in your beliefs, your thoughts, how you show up and how you were able to create this phenomenal business?

S: It stems from knowing that all the power and all the sustenance comes from God ultimately. It is said that the companions noticed that the prophet the way that he used to rely on God, it would lead you to think that he did not do any preparation for what he was setting out to do but when they saw the way that he prepares, it would lead one to think that he had no reliance on God. Meaning that whatever major task he was working on, it looked like he had no reliance on God to prepare so much so that perhaps he was banking on his hard work and the proof of his efforts but then if you saw the way he relied on God, you would see that maybe he has not done any preparation for what he is trying to accomplish. Ultimately all success comes from God, but you have to do your part and go out and work like a maniac and have a much disciplined work ethic to be a business person or an entrepreneur.

One of the keys for me is waking up super early to pray my morning prayers and right after that, a lot of people stop here, even religious people go back to bed and await the 8 am an alarm clock. What you should do is hop into the shower and get your rear end in your office and start working. The Prophet made a pray that he asked God to bless his Peoples in the early hours. The early hours are super dark and quiet where almost no other soul will bother you and if you start with the mindset that I am going to work and I have a goal, you can get a ton of work done. That is another big thing. You have to have goals that are written out. Everybody talks about it but nobody does it. Write them out on a tangible piece of paper and adhere to the steps that will lead you to those goals and the sky is the limit with what you can accomplish.

For example one of my goals this year is to work with the WAFA House. They are an organization here in New Jersey that caters to women sufferers of domestic violence. It was founded by Muslims but caters to all women who have had to undergo such a tragic experience. You won't hear their stories from the tabloids, and nobody talks about it. Thankfully there's an organization that addresses it and I genuinely believe in the work that they doing, and the good they are trying to spread. What I want to do is make so much money this year so that I can take a house, renovate it, and donate it to them free of charge with all taxes paid off for the first year as it's given to them. That's one of my goals. It's what drives me, what gets me up in the morning is; that if I don't do this then there are a group of women who aren't going to have a house or a shelter that they can go to if they are in this sort of situation in their life. After a certain point, it's not about you anymore, but more about us to serving humanity and that's ultimately what we are truly taking home with us at the end of the day. I could have a million dollars and it does me no good because it's not going to follow me into my grave. What is going to follow me is the money I use to help others around me in the world. One of the things that we're very passionate about is orphan funding. Today we currently sponsor 11 orphans and our goal is to sponsor another 10 this year. Each year as our revenue grows; we want to build that up to 100 orphans. Why not?

I mean the Prophet himself was an orphan and somebody took care of him, and he said that "he who takes care of the orphan will be with me in heaven like this," as he put his middle finger and his index finger together. I want to be with the prophet in the afterlife. If I can do anything and if I had anything to say to myself on the Day of Judgment, I want to use my finances and my resources to be able to do these sorts of things. The only way I am going to be able to do that is if I can build a big company that can generate those kinds of funds. It all ties in together. Your businesses, your family, all of these are tied together and how you go about conducting your life. It starts with a big way and it starts with knowing that God can fulfill or answer any question and make it come to pass but you have to wrack your brain and work strategically, methodically, and consistently to make it come to life and you leave the rest of it to God.

F: If someone is reading this right now, what is the first thing he or she should do if they want to get into this kind of business?

S: The first thing is to get educated about it and learn it like anything else. If you want to learn medicine or become a doctor, you would have to go to medical school. If you want to actively pursue real estate investing and do exactly what I do, you should find a local mentor. By the way, we offer mentor programs. You can find someone to teach you the ropes or even offer your services for free and go work for them and learn it that way. The other is you have to decide if you have no time to do this or the money, then what you should do is become a pattern investor and find somebody that can get you those services where they can park your money and invest it for you into conservative but good yielding, high yielding real estate services.

Those are the two ways you have to think about. You got to first take inventory of yourself to see if you have time on your hands. If you have time, then you can learn how to flip houses and invest in rental properties. If you don't have time, then you can just invest passively and if you have neither time nor money, you could learn a strategy called wholesale within the real estate market, which you can pick up and learn pretty quickly. There are tons of books about it as well. I have read copious amounts of books about it and did a lot of wholesaling to get me started. That's a strategy that you can do if you are dead broke and you have no services and no time. This is a business that you need time for. If you have 10-15 hours a week then you can earn $10,000 on your first deal. Also, I make myself very accessible to potential investors and beginners who want to learn more about all of this.

My email is smalik@strategicrealtyllc.com. If you have any questions or if you are looking for any guidance in real estate, don't hesitate to reach out to me.

F: Wonderful! Can anyone contact you on Facebook? Besides your email address?

S: Yes, just send me a message on Facebook. You can find me on LinkedIn. My name is somewhat unique even within the Muslim population. You'll be able to find me pretty easy on both these sites and can get a response reasonably quickly as I am active on both platforms.

F: Thank you for your time. It's been very educational.

S: Thanks for having me.

ABOUT THE AUTHOR

Shomail Malik, like most Pakistanis, was conceived by his parents to become a doctor. Where he comes from, you have two choices: become a doctor or an engineer. If you dare pick anything else, you just might get disowned. While on his pre-med journey in college, he started his own business by partnering with an Internet service provider and became one of the top distributors in the entire  country. He told his parents that he would no longer be pursuing medicine because his heart inclined towards having his own business. Around this time in 2002, as he was entering his last year in college, he was introduced into the world of real estate by a good friend and went on to get his real estate license and then become a real estate agent with Keller Williams. He credits much of his success to his broker and mentor in those days, Mr. Mohammad Abbasi.

Determined to make this parent proud, he graduated from Rutgers College in 2003 with a degree in Economics and minor in Neuroscience and went off to work for Procter & Gamble Pharmaceuticals in the sales division. He spent 11 years working for pharmaceutical and medical supplies companies, earning numerous promotions and sales awards along the way. In 2008, while still employed, and as the economy began its downward spiral, he started Strategic Realty Solutions (www.strategicrealtyllc.com), a real estate investment and residential re-development company that acquires distressed properties, rehabs them, and sells them to retail and landlord buyers. In 2010, while working his full-time 9-to-5 and running a full-time business, he began his graduate work pursuing an Executive MBA at Rutgers Business School. In his last position, while working in Corporate America, he was the Global Business Manager for a $35 business unit at a Fortune 500 healthcare company. Finally, in March 2014, as his real estate investment firm grew exponentially, he left Corporate America once and for all.

Along with his success in real estate investing, Shomail is often called upon to speak at regional and national real estate conferences throughout the country. He is one of the nation's foremost experts in wholesaling, rehabbing, raising private capital, short sales, bank-owned properties, and turnkey rental properties. In 2012, he started Real Estate Wealth Academy (www.REWealthAcademy.com), a premier education company that teaches and provides support to real estate investors all over the country. Additionally, Shomail also runs a thriving real estate club, NJ Real Estate Connect, which meets monthly in Central NJ, where he brings other movers and shakers in the real estate investing industry to share case studies and best practices with his audience members.

Shomail is very involved in his community and humanitarian work. He also delivers the Friday sermon at the weekly congregational prayers at various mosques throughout NJ. He lives with his wife and three kids in Franklin Park, NJ. Shomail can be contacted directly via email at smalik@strategicrealtyllc.com

Facebook
Facebook.com/Shomail.Malik

Notes: ✍

Notes:

FATIMA OMAR KHAMISSA

"Writing a bestselling book gives you instant credibility and authority in your niche. It's a very clever marketing tool"

Platinum Publishing

The clients that we help at Platinum Publishing are business owners, entrepreneurs, and professionals who want to double and triple their business. If you are tired of being your city's best-kept-secret and you've decided that you want to publish a book because publishing a book is a very clever marketing tool to get your business noticed - You could use your book as a business card.

Platinum Publishing also helps people write legacy books. Grandparents, great grandparents, aunts, uncles, parents who want to leave their legacy behind. This is important for children and families to know their life didn't get started at a certain hospital where they were born. These kids have a legacy that is rich and fulfilling.

I would love to have a written documentation of my family's history. My grandparents from my fathers-side were born in the same village as Gandhi. In the time of partition, they left on the ships from India to South Africa. My parents were born in South Africa. They got involved with the anti-apartheid movement. For me to have this kind of history, written and documented, would be incredibly liberating to share this with my family. That's the beauty of having a legacy book.

I had already published three of my own books. You can find them on Amazon. The first one is called *What is the Verbal Abuse*. The second one is called *Fearless Faith* and the third one is called *50 Ways to Brand Yourself Online for Free*. After publishing these books – nothing happened. They sat on Amazon and not many people benefitted from them. I was extremely frustrated. I didn't know what to do about it. I spent a long time writing these books, editing, proofreading, getting graphics done for them and I had to find a system that worked.

I met a couple of book coaches at a conference in Texas. They said they could teach me how to do bestsellers. I was hooked. We worked together for about 18 months teaching me how Amazon works, how best sellers work, and the different criteria that is needed to create a best seller.

There are three parts to the equation of a successful book launch.

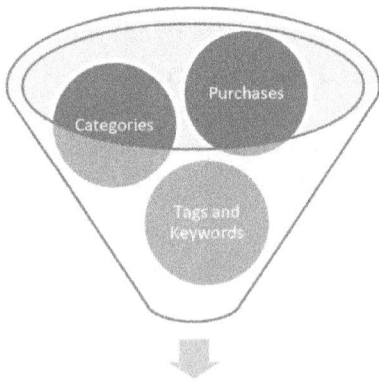

BESTSELLER

1. Number of Purchases.

2. Categories.

3. Keywords.

When you get the right formula, you get a best seller.

In 2015, my niche market was divorced Muslim woman. In February of that year, I wrote *How to be a Muslim Woman Divorced and Totally Confident.* That book hit number-one in 24 hours. In November of the same year, I wrote *From Ex to Extraordinary* and that book became a best seller as well.

I quickly realized the power of having a best seller. My annual income became my monthly income and --- not from the sale of books. People wanted to coach with me and I didn't even have a coaching program. I was invited to speak on panels as an expert at conferences globally. I got so busy, I had to get a loan to pay people to babysit my kids because some of the money was still coming in. After that, people in my circles, who were not coaches or trainers asked me how I successfully published TWO bestsellers in the same year. They had been trying and they didn't know the formula. I said, "We could do that for you" and the publishing company was born - how awesome.

One of the most common misconceptions about publishing is that you're going to get rich from selling books or that publishing a book is a retirement plan. That is a pitfall. You've got to get your mindset correct -- selling books is not going to be a retirement plan and you're not going to get rich from the selling of the books. However, having a book opens doors that that may have been closed previously.

Imagine going to an expensive fundraising dinner. The Master of Ceremonies introduces the speaker as *published author Fatima Omar* or they say *best-selling author, Fatima Omar.* What is your perception of the speaker?

> In this world -- labels matter. People have a certain perception of a best-selling author. They immediately trust you to know the subject-matter. The difference being a published author versus a best-selling author is HUGE. You're not going to get rich from the direct sale of books, but you are going to change the perception of how society sees you as an advocate, and an educator in your niche. And that's going to change your bank account.

How do we help clients get bestseller status?

Our agency, Platinum Publishing is part of a conglomerate of 300 global agencies. Our only mandate is to help our clients get to bestseller. You never have to worry about begging your friends and family or social media contacts to purchase books.

You never have to worry about purchasing a thousand books to keep in your garage.

One of my clients had to do that with another publishing company. Two weeks later, she had a flood. All her books were ruined. This is terrible. I wish she had spoken to me before this happened.

What we do as publishing consultants:

- We share our exact system.

- We share our propriety template.

- We share our intellectual property.

- We share our step by step guides.

- We share our knowledge.

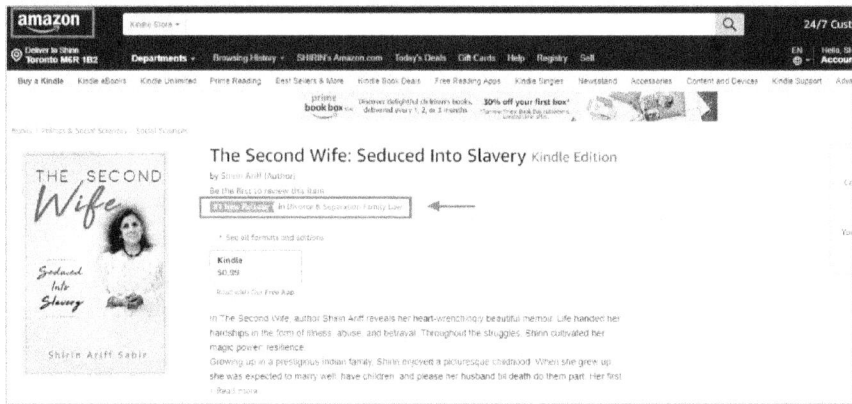

Most of our clients are non-writers. They are professionals, entrepreneurs, speakers, mortgage agents, chiropractors, accountants, chefs, cooks, moms, dads, and people from all walks of life.

But they are not necessarily writers.

In our program, we help you every step of the way. We coach you, we hold your hand, and we have multiple different packages that fits your needs.

One of my clients Mary, already has a book. She uploaded it a couple of years ago and it's been sitting on Amazon doing nothing. She gave me a call and said "Hey Fatima, I have a book already. We uploaded it a couple of years ago and it just didn't do anything. Can you help us?"

Yes absolutely.

We go into your back-office, we change the tags, the categories, and the keywords. We may also get a new graphic. We do a best seller launch. And voila!

She's got that status because once a best seller, you're always a best seller. That title can never be taken away from you.

We help you avoid all the obstacles. There are three phases from start to finish.

1. Phase one. We coach you through the entire process of extracting the book. We share our intellectual property and

guide you through the writing. We set up coaching calls. Once you get the content, we go on to phase two.

2. Phase two is the editing, the proofreading, the graphics and the best seller launch on Kindle Amazon. Once all the testing is done, we do the book launch. We wait for Amazon to call us a bestseller. Once Amazon calls you a best seller, we send you all the screenshots as proof. We write a press release which gets picked up by NBC, CBC, and Fox etc.

3. Phase three is the printing of the physical books. We can now ethically take a "bestselling logo" and stick it on the cover. This makes your cover look magnetic and irresistible. We print the physical books. We have it shipped to you.

Best part, you keep ALL the royalties. Being in the industry, I learned that royalties only benefits the publisher and it handcuffs the author to the publisher. I wanted to create freedom for my clients. You keep all the Royalties.

We also guarantee the book will hit TOP 10 as a best seller. We show you how to work the back office where you can order your own books at wholesale price. Then we give you the keys to the car and we show you how to change your password. It's all set up for you. You can order books at the wholesale price, and anyone anywhere in the world can order a book and it'll get delivered to them. It's pretty awesome.

My Journey into Publishing

I'm pretty new in the publishing world. It's only been five years. Before that, I was a homeschool mom-of-five, I didn't work outside the home. It was my husband's job to bring home the deer and that relationship didn't work out. I found myself in a position where I had to feed my family and keep them safe. I learned to rely on my Creator and to surrender.

I immersed myself in courses on self-development, I know that the more I change and transform, the better I get to show up as my authentic self.

Well let's talk about failure, I actually coined a term called 'FFF' (Fail, Forward, Faster). I was the student who got 97% consistently, and my wonderful late father would say "what did you do with the other three percent honey?" I realized that he was doing the best he could because he thought education was the key to success and to my father, education that was everything. But when I stepped into the entrepreneurship world, I learned very quickly that it's not perfection we are looking for. If you keep on working on your business, failure is a BIG part of the journey. I had to change my mind to fall in love with failing. Don't take ourselves too seriously and just keep moving towards your target. It will work out. Strive for consistent and persistent rather than perfection.

What would I say to my younger self? I would say to her: "Lighten up, things are not so serious. Ask a lot of questions and learn to ask for things. Learn to ask for time, learn to ask for money, learn to ask for a massage, and learn to ask for time". That's what I would say to my younger self.

The habits question. I do a lot of different habits; I wake up in the morning, do my prayers. I read sacred scripture every morning - that sets my day up. I journal, I meditate at least twice a day, every day and I walk in the evenings. I'm reading three or four books right now and that's part of my habit.

One of the best piece of advice I would give if someone is considering writing a book is to have a call with me. That's the best way we are going to figure it out. Go to speakwithfatima.com. Book a time so we can get on a call. Let's figure out if you have a book in you and, if you and I make a good fit. That's the first step.

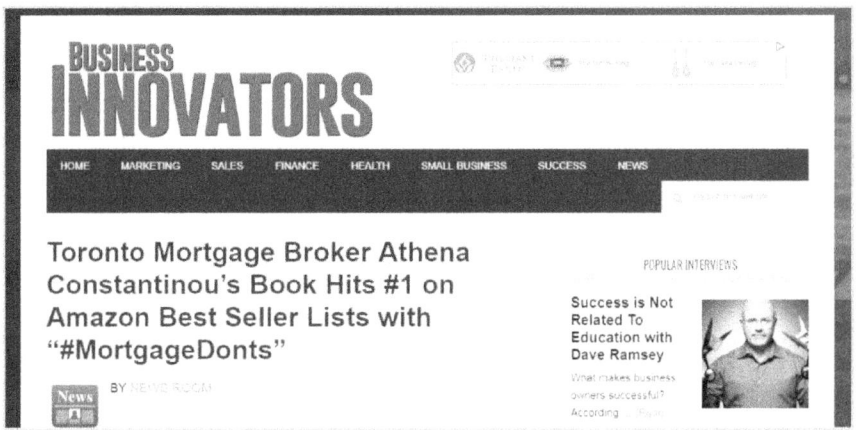

If you're saying, "I don't have much money to invest." I would say, "Write your book. Write as much as you can. You might not need us to help you, or coach you through the entire process. Once you are done writing, we will come in at the very end. Maybe proofread, edit, do the graphics and then the best seller launch for you".

The most important thing that you should think about is *do the book now.* There is no time like now to do the book because time is not on your side.

What makes us really different is,

1. We keep ZERO royalties. You will have the keys to the car. You'll be able to print books as you want. You'll have wholesale pricing for the rest of your life and most publishers don't do that.

2. We guarantee you will be at the top 10 and I can promise you, it's very challenging for you to do this by yourself.

How do you contact me?

Go to this site SpeakWithFatima.com

To conclude, I can tell you that you probably have multiple books in you. You might be thinking well, I have a solo book or maybe I just want a chapter in a book. You can be part of a book just like this one; maybe you're a speaker and you want to be in a book. Maybe you're a healer and you want to be in a book. Maybe you are an entrepreneur, maybe you're in real estate - contact us, we're very flexible and we like challenges. We like being curious and creative, working with different people to create beautiful things. Give us a shout and I look forward to speaking with you.

NEWSCENTER

HOME   NEWS   WEATHER   SPORTS   COMMUNITY   NC1 FEATUR

Coach and Mentor, Fatima Omar Khamissa's book, Million Stars, Hits Number One on Amazon

Posted: Nov 30, 2017 6:01 AM EST

Best-selling author and success coach, Fatima Omar Khamissa, pulls back the curtain on the coaching industry in her new best-selling book, Million Stars: Changing Lives, Finding Freedom, Building Personal Power.

Million Stars: Changing Lives, Finding Freedom, Building Personal Power, is breaking barriers for women, and pulling-back-the-curtain on how to launch a successful on-line and off-line coaching business.

When interviewed, Omar Khamissa, said "the book, was written as an introduction to The Million Stars Certification Program This is a coaching-certification-program for one million women, globally regardless of race, religion, ethnicity or background to create an online platform to coach, make money, and have freedom of choice."

FATIMA'S BIO

For 21 years, Fatima Omar Khamissa was a victim of an abusive marriage which destroyed all the hopes and dreams she had for herself.

She took her five children and left that marriage and today, Fatima is the CEO of Fatima Omar International Inc., leading provider of training, coaching and publishing for women who feel stuck, frustrated, and tired of living lives without satisfaction, meaning, and progress.

The trauma of abuse, apartheid and violence was not able to break Fatima's spirit and as an international best-selling author, Fatima is sharing her message to inspire, motivate, and lead women all over the world to continual growth in both personal and professional life.

She has written 6 books, three became bestsellers on Amazon.com. After writing her books, her annual income became her monthly income and her publishing company was born. To date, she has helped more than 67 people become bestselling authors through her publishing company.

She uses psychology and brand awareness techniques to position her clients as authorities and thought-leaders in their niche. Fatima is known for her "out-of-the-box" ideas to empower, educate and inspire audiences globally. Business owners choose Fatima, because she is not "just another coach", instead she's a real business strategist and thought leader who creates custom plans for you that details practical strategies for overcoming obstacles and unlock your greatest abilities.

Fatima Omar International Inc. is a boutique personal branding firm specializing in publishing, certified coach training and press releases to create visibility, authority and expert status for their clients

They shine the spotlight on you. Their custom packages are uniquely created for you and they guarantee best seller status so you can use your bestselling book as a business card to attract higher paying clients and global speaking gigs, to make a difference and make more money.

They equip you with transforming your past pain and skills into purpose, power, and profit through coach certification training. Fatima's step-by-step guides and templates take all the guesswork out of your entrepreneurship journey in order to attract clients while you are being certified.

A third-party testimonial from a journalist that is featured on ABC, NBC, Fox, etc. is a powerful platform to create brand awareness and to catapult you into a sphere of leadership. Press releases give you instant credibility and show the world that you are the person that they should be working with.

Contact Fatima and her extraordinary team at
SpeakwithFatima.com today.

The world needs your skills and expertise

Notes: ✍

Notes: ✍

Other books by:

Fatima Omar Khamissa
& Platinum Publishing

Property Trendsetters:
Successful Toronto Real estate Experts Share Key Insider-Secrets

#MortgageDonts by Athena Constantinou

The Second Wife by Shirin Ariff

Brilliance: Health and Wellness Industry Experts Share
Their Insider Secrets, Experience and Advice on Healing

Million Stars Changing Lives, Finding Freedom
and Building Personal Power

How to be a Muslim Woman,
Divorced and Totally Confident

From Ex to Extraordinary – How to Make Your
Divorce A Springboard for Excellence

Fearless Faith

50 Ways to Brand Yourself
Online for Free

What is Verbal Abuse

To contact Fatima and her team at Platinum Publishing

Send an email to info@FatimaOmarKhamissa.com

www.ingramcontent.com/pod-product-compliance
Lightning Source LLC
Chambersburg PA
CBHW060828170526
45158CB00001B/109